"Ali Lara's *Digesting Reality* brilliantly and wisely returns human activities, such as eating and drinking, to the theoretical landscape focused on the other-than-human. Using a surprisingly fresh, multilayered, analytic approach to process and objects applied in fascinating case studies, *Digesting Reality* is a delicious read."

– Professor Patricia Ticineto Clough, PhD, LP

"Ali Lara's *Digesting Reality* capaciously explores the complex political ecologies of bodies-in-relations far from equilibrium. His analyses of multiscalar processes affecting objects, subjects, and ecologies draws on cutting-edge work in neuroscience, social psychology, and critical theory to question and move beyond the habits of thoughts tied to a Eurocentric anthropocene. His finely intercalated researches affirm in surprising and insightful ways the 'pre-individual knowing' so crucial today in the ongoing renewal of the project of decolonizing affect. We will all need to be reading him in the years to come!"

– Amit S. Rai, author of *Untimely Bollywood* and *Jugaad Time*

"Here's a whole new methodological recipe for doing food studies in the 21st century! Ali Lara shows, chapter by chapter, how to fold multiple theory ingredients together – process philosophy, object-oriented ontology, affect studies, speculative realism, new materialism, actor network theory, and more – and, then, serve them up through a set of very substantive and tasty case studies: tacos, chocolate, wine, mezcal, living as a vegan. Your everyday practices of eating and drinking will never quite feel the same after digesting the contents of this truly groundbreaking work."

– Dr. Gregory J. Seigworth, co-editor of *The Affect Theory Reader* and co-editor of *Capacious: Journal for Emerging Affect Inquiry*

Decentering Subjectivity in Everyday Eating and Drinking

This important book offers a model to analyze the configurations of reality as manifested in everyday practices of eating and drinking in relation to the development of human subjectivity. The author uses concrete examples from daily life related to eating and drinking habits, such as "eating tacos" or "taking a shot of mezcal", to offer an interface of interaction between body/mind and material entities connecting all scales of reality.

Borrowing scientific insights from molecular biology and neuroscience, combined with a touch of decolonial spirit, the author examines specific "processes" and/or "objects" triggered by eating and drinking events, such as the production of heat as you eat a taco, or the interchange of knowledge while drinking mezcal. The book develops an approach to human subjectivity informed by material and aesthetic encounters beyond the analysis of language, representation, and social structures and aims to contribute to the contemporary landscape of efforts decentering our understanding of both human and nonhuman affairs.

With its multidimensional exploration of our relationship with food, this is thought-provoking reading for scholars and students in critical psychology, philosophy, and the social sciences.

Ali Lara received his PhD in social psychology from the Autonomous University of Barcelona and was previously a postdoctoral fellow at the City University of New York. He currently works as a lecturer in psychology at the University of East London. His research interests revolve around speculative philosophy-based theories such as affect and Object Oriented Ontology, social studies of the body and the senses, and decolonial theory.

Concepts for Critical Psychology: Disciplinary Boundaries Re-thought
Series editor: Ian Parker

Developments inside psychology that question the history of the discipline and the way it functions in society have led many psychologists to look outside the discipline for new ideas. This series draws on cutting edge critiques from just outside psychology in order to complement and question critical arguments emerging inside. The authors provide new perspectives on subjectivity from disciplinary debates and cultural phenomena adjacent to traditional studies of the individual.

The books in the series are useful for advanced level undergraduate and postgraduate students, researchers and lecturers in psychology and other related disciplines such as cultural studies, geography, literary theory, philosophy, psychotherapy, social work and sociology.

Most recently published titles:

Rethinking Education through Critical Psychology
Cooperative schools, social justice and voice
Gail Davidge

Developing Minds
Psychology, neoliberalism and power
Elise Klein

Marxism and Psychoanalysis
In or against Psychology?
David Pavón-Cuéllar

Decentering Subjectivity in Everyday Eating and Drinking
Digesting Reality
Ali Lara

For more information about this series, please visit: www.routledge.com

Decentering Subjectivity in Everyday Eating and Drinking

Digesting Reality

Ali Lara

Routledge
Taylor & Francis Group
LONDON AND NEW YORK

First published 2021
by Routledge
2 Park Square, Milton Park, Abingdon, Oxon OX14 4RN

and by Routledge

605 Third Avenue, New York, NY 10017

Routledge is an imprint of the Taylor & Francis Group, an informa business

British Library Cataloguing-in-Publication Data
A catalogue record for this book is available from the British Library

Library of Congress Cataloging-in-Publication Data
A catalog record for this book has been requested

ISBN 13: 978-0-367-53490-5 (hbk)
ISBN 13: 978-0-367-53485-1 (pbk)
ISBN 13: 978-1-003-08219-4 (ebk)

Typeset in Bembo
by Apex CoVantage, LLC

Contents

Acknowledgments

Everyone who has ever shared food or a drink with me deserves a thank-you; it has been in those kinds of moments when I have gotten most of the inspiration for this book. I think I first imagined this book eating *tacos de costilla* with Jessica Assai in the streets of Mexico City and kept imagining – although not yet writing it – during my last years as a PhD student in Barcelona. Most of the content of this book was actually thought and written in New York during my postdoctoral years in the City University of New York. For all the support during those years, her generosity in sharing knowledge, the inspiration, and the very way my mind has been shaping, I thank Patricia Clough. Thanks to my colleagues and friends in our affect research group for making space to grow together, Akemi Nishida, Wen Liu, Rachel Liebert, Colin Ashley, and Michelle Billies. For the time spent together and the good memories, thank you, Jen Tang, Giazu Enciso, Fernando Quigua, Alyson Spurgas, Sandra Moyao, and Bibi Calderon. During the years I have been trying to write in English, a lot of generous people have helped me editing my work; you have no idea how important you were and how much I owe you, Alexis Larsson, Michelle Billies, Fernando Quigua, Tehseen Noorani, Rachel Liebert, Omar Montana, and Isabella Mighetto.

The final sections of the book were written in London in my new job in the University of East London, where I thank my new friends and colleagues Sophia Bokhari, Stephanie Davis, Rachel Liebert, and Ian Tucker for all their support that allowed me to finish the book. For the inspiration, conversations, and all the support in different moments, thank you, Gregory Seigworth, Melissa Gregg, Jane Bennett, Paul Stenner, Steve Brown, Tony Sampson, and my friend Amit Rai. Thank you.

For the pictures in Chapter 1 thanks to Sofia Cruz and to Jorge Mendoza for being the model. To Jen Tang, for sharing indulgences and taking me to the chocolate room that was hugely inspirational for Chapter 3 and for having that bottle of zinfandel with me that became the momentum that inspired Chapter 4. To all vegans who helped me think about the politics of veganism but specially Rachel Liebert and Ingrid Bernhardt. To all the people who drank and became poems by my side, making possible Chapter 5: Kuriko Ishikawa, Jessica Assai, Tehseen Noorani, Lorena Cueva, Angelica Vázquez, Iris Monroy, Ozuany Mugica, thank you for the mezcal encounters and thank you for the poetry. I want to give a big thank you to my friend Omar Perez, aka "el Tellez", for partnering up with me and making Tay Ñuu a place for poetry.

Thanks in Buenos Aires to Cecilia Macon, who invited me to keynote at the international conference "thinking affect", where I shared an early version of what here appears as the multilayered model, and also thank you to Ana Abramowski and Cynthia Francica for the conversations that enriched the Buenos Aires experiences and my work. A very early version of Chapter 1 was presented in Mexico at the ENAH, back in 2013, thanks to an invitation from my friends and colleagues Jorge Mendoza and Juan Soto. A later version was presented at the authority network conference in New York, where I met one of the organizers, Tehseen Noorani, who would become my dear friend and years later would help me also come up with the title of the book. Thank you also to my friend Antar Martiez for all the conversations and for inviting me several times to University of Colima in Mexico to share my research; a very early version of Chapter 5 was presented there. Thanks also to Eduardo Rodriguez, who trained me as an undergrad and invited me in 2017 to share some of the main ideas contained in the introduction of the book in the University of Puebla, Mexico.

Very importantly, I want to thank Mexico for being such a mind-blowing matrix of flavors and sensations that have inspired me for years. With Mexico comes family, and I want to thank my sisters Aranza and Maritza for just loving me and letting me cook for them and eating with me, and my mother Rocio, the person who fed me and taught me to eat, to crave the world, and to go and eat it. Chapter 1 was originally published by The Senses and Society, Chapter 3 by Capacious journal of Affect inquiry, Chapter 4 by Subjectivity, thanks to all three journals and the corresponding editors for allowing the reprinting.

Finally, there is nothing at all to thank the Mexican council of science CONACYT, which in different moments refused to support my research and did not help me get back to my country. I hope other young researchers will cope despite the lack of support that you provide.

Preface

"You are what you eat" is one popular phrase that the discipline of psychology has found difficult to digest. This is partly because the discipline, which is so busy turning human subjects into objects, actually shrinks with distaste from what is most material about our existence, the fact that we ingest material from our environment, put it in one end of our bodies, and then expel the leftovers, jettisoning what is not useful from the other end. How we do that, and how we relate to the process of selecting, comparing, and sharing the stuff we busily feed on, is the topic of this book, and its touchstone is precisely what would help us understand better why psychology cannot handle food affects. It is affect that is crucial here, not the standardised array of "emotions" that comprise the reduced table of senses that psychology textbooks sample and theorize about, usually confined to sections devoted to "emotion and motivation".

This is a book to savour. Take it slowly; treat the experience of reading it as being at one with the "slow food" to which a significant class layer is invited to ask for when they use their valuable leisure time in such a way as to distinguish themselves from the time-poor working people who have to make do with fast food. The book speaks of the different worlds in which we enjoy eating and how we try to safeguard those parts of our lives that have been subject to industrialisation. We are increasingly disconnected from the food we eat; it becomes alien to us at the moment it is packaged in such a way as to make it all the more tempting to eat. Industrialisation of food mirrors the industrialisation of psychology; this book has deep, profound implications for both: for how to resist both forms of disconnection and to connect with what we eat and who we are once again. This book needs to be taken slowly because the theoretical journey is necessarily as complicated as the many kinds of cuisine we encounter today in the world. And the construction process is as complex in the world of theory as it is in the world of food. Although psychology avidly attempts to simplify human experience, and to break it down into quantifiable components in its experimental studies, the actual experience and affect of being human is many faceted and difficult to enjoy in one course or in one sitting.

Digesting Reality: Practice, Process, Objects is a methodological as well as conceptual challenge to psychology, engaging in a kind of critique that addresses the reader as a gourmand, turns them into someone who will think about their food and what they do with it in a very different way, and along the way, learn something about aspects of their own "psychology" that the discipline industrialises. Let us take our lead from Ali Lara's detailed conceptual analysis of food and our relation to food and acknowledge that the world of food shows us how contradictory and enjoyable it is to be human. This book will take you back from the objects that psychology trades in to affect-suffused subjects, us, those who are inside psychology but still must leave it from time to time, usually three times a day, to sustain ourselves, whether that is in our individual kitchens or shared cafeterias. To take food into psychology is therefore to be "out with" it. But, careful, if you eat too much of this book at once, you will make yourself a bit dizzy and be tempted to regurgitate it over your friends, to tell them about it, a sign of what rich fare it is indeed.

Ian Parker
University of Manchester

Digesting reality

It is Friday night in Mexico City. We got off the subway and stood on the street, wondering where to go to get drunk. The streets had this massive lighting that made us feel at the center of the stage, as if the city were glowing just for us. The city flowed fast, crazy as always. But the polluted air still had time to caress our faces, to say, "Welcome *valedor*". Her smile gave her away; the way mine responded betrayed us both. "My place", she suddenly said with the sweetest voice. So, there we were, arm in arm, walking to her place. A few steps further and that sweet voice softly sighed, "Let's have a tiny sin!". And we were sitting in the street chairs before the end of the phrase. – *De qué va a querer sus tacos patrona?* a waiter asked. We stopped for some rib tacos. I couldn't say no because I got seduced myself by the smell of the ribs and deeply understood her need to "sin". I felt it. It was a sin mostly because we were supposed to have dinner later, but the feeling was stronger than us. It was a place with tables and chairs spread on the sidewalk, decorated in white and blue stripes. Some objects in the street were painted in blue, with the same paint from inside: light poles, bollards, and trashcans. There was no "white" outside, just blue, as if the "white" of outside were the city itself, with its hustle and bustle, and the always caring air. Street lights were falling over the blue paint; the air was filled by street noises; expansive rib smells moved by heat and cooking fumes; and of course her sweet voice telling me about her salsa preferences. While we were eating a drop of sweat was born from her forehead, shining with the lights, hiding behind the fumes, and falling like a waterfall framing her face. Wasn't she beautiful? She smiled, the drop deviated to her neck, and we kept eating. The tacos were amazing; they entered our bodies with the ease of someone who has been there before. When we finished eating, she had this sparkle of glee in her eyes and made a knowing smile that let me know: our sin was consummated. Our lethargic bodies made a last effort; we stood up and continued walking to her place.

This is a field note from 2013, and it's also the experience that triggered the idea for this book: a moment of overwhelming awareness of the complexity of the event, sure. I am especially overwhelmed by the concatenation and emergence of events that leave footprints as experiences but also leave their mark in material events and ultimately in the bodies dwelling in this world. We stopped by to get some tacos, and thousands of traces came to claim other presences: the knowing of how of the city redirected our paths; the catholic reference and the shame consubstantial of pleasure; whatever was happening inside her body and how it culminated in that drop of sweat; the emotions that emerged near to the heat and the way they reflected our history of precarity; the atmosphere half city, half *taqueria*; the local evolution of the organisms turning a tongue on fire into pleasure where others feel pain; the politics and economics of street food and the way they shape our bodies; the words of the waiter carrying the history of colonization and transformation of our bodies; the taco itself as a miracle of creativity. How amazing it was to see that our ways of living and understanding the world are shaped by little moments like that one and that in those little moments different parts of the world, from the chili to the street noise, were sending their contributions to our lives to keep shaping. How amazing it was to realize the untimely temporality of the event, able of opening up the history through the irrefutable evidence of the shapes of our bodies.

That was the triggering moment when I started to think that I wanted to analyze the ways in which human subjectivity is shaped by human practices but that such practices should be looked at by including all the activity that they carry forward in different scales of the reality and different aesthetic encounters at stake in a practice so simple, like eating a street taco, and that therefore the study of subjectivity must be the study of the material transformation of bodies. From the cells in the body encountering the swallowed food, to the words being said, to the history of a country, all this shapes matter, like bodies and cities, and shapes cultures as well, subjectivities, and ultimately the world we live in. When we do something reality crosses through us and transforms us in material, symbolic, political, and aesthetic forms at all different levels, and as we live, we are being and becoming, creating our pacts with the world and the ways in which we get to incorporate such a world. As we live, we are constantly digesting reality, not as a metaphor for comprehending or making sense of it but as an actual ontological and material transformation caused by a metabolic merging process between us and the world.

I managed to make some notes that day after the tacos, and that was the start of this book and the idea of creating a proposal for an analytical approach to reality as manifested through the everyday practices of eating and drinking. To carry on with that agenda, *Digesting Reality* looks at concrete events such as "eating a taco" or "drinking a *jicara* of mezcal" to explore the emergent configurations of different scales of organization of life. The book accomplishes this proposal through the analysis of specific "processes" and "objects" triggered by these eating/drinking practices, such as the production of heat as you eat a taco or the interchange of knowledge between plants and humans while drinking mezcal.

The model, which I will be calling a multilayered model during the rest of the book, is half based on description of the processes and objects involved in the practice and half based on speculation about the relations among what I call different scales and different aesthetic dimensions of reality. Thus, this book presents an empirico-speculative approach for a multiscalar and multidimensional analysis of human practices. The main strategy of this approach is an epistemic one, namely, redefining the notion of practice as an ecological event triggering activity and patterns of activity within at least three different scales of the reality –"molecular", "organic", and "cultural". Simultaneously, practices trigger encounters among the qualities of the objects involved in that practice, animating an aesthetic dimension of reality, which I analyze by featuring a typology of objects: "haptic objects", "aesthetic objects", and "prosthetic objects". This way of analysis of the material and social reality is the main contribution of this book, an approach in which the analysis of everyday practices becomes the analysis of emergent process and objects within this multiscalar and multidimensional reality. I follow that strategy to construct a model that starts with human affairs but extends all the way to molecular configurations, cultural arrangements, environments, neurological networks, and cosmogonies of existence. This strategy contributes to produce an epistemological and theoretical approach to reality consistent with flat ontologies proposed in contemporary continental perspectives in philosophy.

The speculative nature of this project as well as its philosophical basis come from current debates within the tradition of continental philosophy grouped under the umbrella of speculative realism, from which some of the current trends in social theory such as affect studies, new materialism, or post-human studies have acquired philosophical inspiration. In the last years, these trends in social theory have staged an ontological debate mainly focused on whether it is "processes" or "objects" that should be at the center of social thought. This debate is rooted in philosophical perspectives such as the so-called process philosophies with authors like James, Deleuze, Bergson, or Whitehead and other more recent schools of thought such as object-oriented ontologies mainly proclaimed by Harman, Morton, Bryant, and Bogost. Both of them, process and object philosophies, set the philosophical basis for the theoretical and methodological contribution of this project: to study practices through the altering and combined analysis of objects and processes.

The descriptive nature of this proposal arises in part from contemporary approaches for qualitative analysis in social sciences, including ethnographic traditions in sociology like actor network theory or sensory studies within cultural theory, but also, from the inclusion of some scientific discourses that are used to describe activity at small strata of reality such as the activity of molecular arrangements, neuronal networks or quantum fields. To do that, this book is also informed by some insights developed in fields like molecular biology, quantum physics, and theories of neuroplasticity. Insights from scientific discourse are brought to the analysis to recognize the relations of organic, biological, and material process within the social ecology of the events, particularly when they participate in the mediation and production of human consciousness, as is the case in neurological processes, or physiological processes involved in the sensorium (like thermoception molecules or smell receptors).

At the center of this proposal lies a twofold concern; first, to produce an analytical model based on flat ontology and capable of including all levels of reality without giving ontological priority to human affairs, and second, to create such a model with the capability of accounting for the nature of human conscious – not as an ontological center for reality but as an object embedded within/and shaped by the ecology of events and practices. The result is a nonhuman-centered understanding of human affairs. It is this twofold purpose that makes necessary bringing the human body to the center of the stage, particularly in its interaction with nonhuman agencies as with the food and drinks. The human body is the house of consciousness as well as the threshold between consciousness and the material world; it is the hot spot to start tracking nodes of connections constituting emerging realities. To track this permanent configuration of reality, the analytical focus needs to be something we do with our bodies where consciousness has different degrees of agency, in this sense that eating and drinking practices offer an interface of interaction between body/mind and material entities connecting all scales of reality, from neural and molecular activity to social and cultural arrangements passing through conscious and organic processes. It is in this vein that my nonhuman-centered understanding of human practices is close to what Mark Hansen (2015) calls postphenomenological phenomenology, except mine is not meant to deal with encounters with technology (in this book) or relations between digital entities and humans. Instead, my perspective deals with encounters between humans and other organic nonhuman entities that are empirically recognizable to a certain extent, such as food and drinks. Therefore, it's safe to say that the reality involved in *Digesting Reality* is rather an analogous reality.

This book presents an analysis of reality that strategically sets some steady coordinates as points of reference for different scales of the reality; simultaneously there are objects crossing through and connecting those scales. I will use the term "aesthetic dimension" to refer to the set of these objects. Throughout the book, we theorize three scales: molecular, organic, and cultural. And there are three kinds of objects that animate the aesthetic dimension: haptic objects, aesthetic objects, and prosthetic objects. The first scale, "molecular", refers to activity among small units of matter, like molecules, neurons, or atoms, that are not empirically recognized by humans unless our contact with them is technologically mediated (like using a microscope). The second scale, "organic", is the scale of the conscious human organism and the objects we can filtrate by experience; this is also the scale in which the practice of eating/drinking starts. The third scale, "cultural", refers to general social arrangements involving institutions, identities, and symbolic and socio-historical processes. Connecting and crossing the three scales of the reality are the aesthetic dimensions animated by objects; the first type of object dwelling in these dimensions are "haptic objects"; these are objects that emerge from an organism and touch other organisms, like smell or texture of the skin. The second type is "aesthetic objects", objects that we consciously recognize and that redirect our regime of perception, like an apple. Finally, the third is "prosthetic objects", objects that amplify the regime of perception as well as the lived experience of a body so it can be felt by other bodies, like a poem. I will expand on this typology of scales and objects later.

Although it is true that this theoretical model drinks and eats from different sources, it is worthy to clarify my standing point. This is not a book on philosophy. I am not a philosopher and wouldn't dare challenge the principles of philosophical perspectives because I don't have the training for such a task. If I borrow and rely on process philosophy and object-oriented ontology (OOO), it is not with the aim to contribute something to them. It is rather to contribute to the adaptation that they require to be useful for the purposes of social sciences and social theory.[1] This is also not a book on science. If I borrow some of the insights developed in quantum physics, organic and molecular biology, or neurosciences it is because to some extent, it is necessary to understand how they work to better grasp the forms in which we inhabit this world. This is a book on social sciences that creates social theory. My contribution therefore is to the contemporary fields of social theory that inspired me and whose discussions I want to enrich, such as those of affect studies, new materialism, and nonhuman studies. I'm a social scientist, and the best I can do is to rely on philosophy and science and adapt some of their principals to the agenda of social theory. Thus, the whole purpose of this book is to create novel social theory that helps to better understand the way we are crossed by reality and what happens to us in the meantime, or as I call it here, the way we are *Digesting Reality*.

Process and objects

Practice, process and objects are, together, my solution toward an understanding of reality that simultaneously accounts for change and stability while rethinking the role and the ways to think about the human in a non-anthropocentric fashion. The gesture of my subtitle is rather simple. This book creates a model to account for reality by analyzing the processes and objects that emerge and are redirected by human practices. This idea has two immediate implications. First, it means a combination of process philosophies and OOO; and second, it involves a reconfiguration of the notion of practice for this concept to work as a matrix of processes and objects. So, let's begin with the philosophical opposition of processes and objects.

Process philosophies have been one of the main gestures of the continental tradition in philosophy during the twentieth century, not that they weren't there before, but at least in what concerns social sciences, the twentieth century was characterized by critical theories' strong enthusiasm to process philosophies mainly through the figure of Guilles Deleuze and the texts he wrote with Felix Guattari but also through Henri Bergson, William James, Gilbert Simondon, and the more recent revival of Alfred North Whitehead.[2] Steve Brown and Paul Stenner (2001) recognize Baruch Spinoza as one common source of inspiration for process philosophers, especially Spinoza's commitment to challenge the body/mind division established by Descartes and that was the core stone of Spinoza's Ethics. According to this argument the object of the idea that constitutes the mind is the body, and therefore, in the mind/body relationship there is no lineal relation of control in any direction but rather an ontological parallelism. "Nobody knows what a body is capable of" became an emblem on the philosophical effort for reducing the privilege of human consciousness in philosophical theories. In a certain way, it is safe to say that all contemporary concerns on the agency of matter, the nonhuman capacities, even the preconscious potentialities of human bodies, represent a heritage that could be tracked to the Spinozist tradition. The focus on the capacities of the bodies became the backdrop for a set of philosophies more interested in what the bodies are becoming than in what they actually are. Thus, Deleuzian becoming, Bergsonian duration, and Whiteheadian prehensions are analytical proposals interested in a processual reality, a reality that is constantly becoming something else.[3]

With the arrival of process philosophies to social sciences in the second half of the twentieth century, a refreshing of critical theories was possible. Critical race theory, feminism, and critical disability studies, among others, found inspiration in the processual understanding of reality that allowed them to keep carrying their agendas. Even more, process philosophies were a condition of possibility for the emergence of some of the latest trends in critical theory such as affect studies (Clough, 2007), new materialism (Coole and Frost, 2010), and nonhuman studies (Grusin, 2015). These trends in social theory have turned our attention to processes that are not consciously controlled or that cannot be consciously perceived, which is important at a time when control mechanisms are operating beyond and beneath human consciousness (like genetic modification of food or different forms of bio-political control). I would go as far as to say that it was the incorporation of process philosophy that allowed social sciences to overcome the obsessions with constructionism, language, and representation that kept them stuck during the 1980s and 1990s, especially by helping social theory place the human body and other materialities at the center of the processual understanding of reality. Deleuze (1988), for example, explains that Spinoza defines bodies in terms of two propositions: one kinetic, according to which "the body is defined by relations of motion and rest, of slowness and speed between particles" (123), and the other dynamic, according to which a body is defined by its capacity to affect and be affected by other bodies. If we take these two propositions, we get a whole processual understanding of the body with internal processes (kinetic) and external relations with other bodies (dynamic). Thus, relations of, within, and among bodies became the currency of critical theories toward the development of a more ontological understanding of human (and otherwise) organisms as a matrix of relations or what Patricia Clough (2008) has called the biomediated body.

There are many common elements in the way process philosophies have been taken up by these three trends in social theory – affect studies, new materialism, and nonhuman studies – but I want to emphasize the fact that the three perspectives carry explicit political agendas. First, affect studies emerged to a large extent as a response to new technological and political devices that brought capitalism to new and sophisticated mechanisms of control in the late twentieth century; see, for example, Clough and Wisley's "Beyond Bio-Politics" (2011) or Massumi's "Ontopolitics" (2015a) for that matter. This is to mention only one of the political faces of the vast literature in affect studies. Second, new materialism, or should I say feminist new materialism, has been responsible for a refreshing expansion of a feminist agenda toward the material realm. Contributions such as Luciana Parisi's "abstract matter", Karen Barad's "agential Realism' (2007), and Jane Bennett's "vital matter" (2010) have expanded feminist theory beyond the epistemological concerns and toward the ontological ones while developing a more sophisticated version of the feminist agenda. Third, nonhuman and/or post-human studies, certainly the youngest of the gang, holds great potential in its promise of non-anthropocentrism, plants, animals, things, and especially the nonhuman within the human hold all the potential for a decolonial project that has been latent since the works of Kohn (2013) or Grusin (2015) and is way more outright in recent contributions like Braidotti (2019). The political charge of these trends in social theory is hugely important because, as we will see shortly, most of the discounters with speculative realism and particularly with OOO can be tracked all the way to these agendas.

Although social theory has enjoyed more than twenty years of process-based contributions and enrichment, in the last ten years new debates within continental philosophy have given birth to so-called speculative realism (Harman, 2018; Bryant, Srnicek and Harman, 2011). Whereas most of the debates of speculative realism remain topics of pure philosophical debate, others have made their way into social sciences and social theory. This is the particular case of OOO. one of the expressions of speculative realism that has been increasingly capturing the attention of scholars in the humanities, arts, and slowly into social sciences. OOO was first proposed by Graham Harman (2005), but the movement has been joined by Levi Bryant (2011), Ian Bogost (2012), and Timothy Morton (2013a, 2013b).

What originally brought together all the exponents of speculative realism was a rejection of what Meillassoux (2008) calls "correlationism", and this refers to the philosophical gesture according to which there is no such thing as a reality independent from human mind because the mere fact of thinking about it makes that reality dependent of human mind. The consequence of correlationism, they claim, has been the development of philosophical perspectives that reduce the nature of reality to what we know about it. Whereas speculative realism and its exponents have different ways to battle correlationism,

Harman has bet for a philosophical model that puts objects at the center of philosophical analysis. For OOO an object is any entity that cannot be reduced (downward) to its components or (upward) to its relations and effects. This principle of nonreduction is applied to all entities in the universe. They are all objects, and although they participate in relations, it is only through their qualities that they engage in such relations. The rest of the object withdraws from the encounter. This proposition has two main consequences: first, that the object is provided with an ontological status that precedes its relations and activity in the world, and second, that we will never have complete access to the full object because some of its qualities do not relate to us (or any other thing). Harman (2011a) developed a philosophical model to explain that some qualities of the objects participate in encounters, of which he calls sensual qualities, and others withdraw from the encounters, to what he calls real qualities. Simultaneously, he claims, objects can be of only two kinds, real objects and sensual objects, both of which withhold the two kinds of qualities. For Harman an object is a cluster of objects containing this fourfold matrix. Timothy Morton (2013a, 2013b) added to OOO two important contributions: the theorization of big, non-localizable objects that he calls hyperobjects, like climate change and the cosmos, and importantly for this book, the idea of vicarious causation that sets the aesthetic dimension as the plane of causality. For Morton, objects can affect only each other's sensual properties because only these properties participate in the encounters; therefore, any alteration of what an object is is an alteration of what this object is for the object that perceives it. It's an aesthetic matter. There is certainly much more to say about OOO, and we will as the book progresses, but for now, I want to go elsewhere. I want to focus on the current debate of whether processes or objects should become the analytical unit and the main ontological unit for the study of life.

One of the foundational books on speculative realism was published under the name of *The Speculative Turn. Continental Materialism and Realism* (Bryant et al., 2011). In that text there is an interchange between Steven Shaviro and Graham Harman on the dispute between processes and objects. Shaviro later would develop a larger version of his contribution and turned it into the second chapter of his interpretation of Whitehead (Shaviro, 2014a). The discussion is based in two points: whether process or object is the one that is useful to account simultaneously for change and stability and the different kind of aesthetics carried in each project. As that discussion goes, Shaviro's Whitehead shares the anti-correlationist commitment of speculative realism, but his strategy is purely relational.

As he puts it, "Whitehead opposes correlationism by proposing a much broader – indeed universally promiscuous – sense of relations among entities" (Shaviro, 2014a, 30). Whereas Whitehead takes individual units, or actual occasions as he calls them, as the ultimate component of reality, he brings relationality as the main quality of such units to give us a world in which entities are embedded in a set of relations with other entities. For Harman, however, this perspective reduces entities in the way in which they are perceived by other entities. For OOO it is the currently unrelated qualities of objects that give the condition of possibility for change and novelty, not the constant dynamic current relations. This is the point upon which Harman rejects Shaviro's criticism. As he contends, "[O]nly a non-relational model of objects is capable of accounting for both the transient and enduring faces of reality. Shaviro denies this, mainly because he wrongly links relations with becoming, and objects with stasis" (Harman, 2011b, 291–292). What we know from this debate is that both Shaviro´s Whitehead and Harman have a place for objects and processes, change, and stability (and both claim that the other's doesn't). As for Whitehead, the actual occasions are the final unit of analysis, whereas its main property is its relationality, and for Harman, the objects have ontological priority, but some of their qualities do relations. It's a matter of ontological precedence that I judge rather irrelevant for the development of social theory.

Later in the debate, Shaviro contrasts Whitehead's treatment of merging properties as an aesthetic phenomenon and Harman's attention to the attraction to withdrawn qualities of an object or what he calls *allure*. For Shaviro, this kind of aesthetics is more of a sublime order. Harman responds to this, claiming that

> Shaviro misses at least two major differences between allure and sublime. First, the sublime is a theory about *human* experience of the world, while allure for me seeps down even into the heart of inanimate matter. . . . Second, in the aesthetics of the sublime the sublime is generally treated as *one*. And here too allure is different, since for me the allure of each object is concretely different.
>
> (Harman, 2011b, 302–303)

Shaviro finds the processual nature of Whitehead's ontology is better prepared to deal with the current changes in the world, like technological invasion or climate change, whereas Harman's OOO is the only one capable of explaining all events in the universe, and he has gone as far as to call it "the new theory of everything" (Harman, 2018). Regardless how they address this matter, the ontological relevance of aesthetics is a second difference/coincidence here.

Even when some discussion of OOO can be found in affect studies, like in Clough (2018) or Sparrow (2014), most of the confrontation and dispute of OOO has come from new materialism, especially in its most feminist expression. Only one year after the Harman-Shaviro debate, in 2012, Graham Harman and Timothy Morton contributed to a special section on "Object-Oriented Literary Criticism" published in the journal *New Literary History*. These contributions were responded to and contested by Jane Bennett, one of the leading authors in new materialism. A little later, in 2015, a version of Harman's and Bennett's contributions was reprinted as part of the edited book *Non-Human Turn* (Grusin, 2015). Interestingly, Bennett's response to Morton and Harman goes in two directions, first addressing their critique of relations as "holisms" and then pointing out to the ethical and political implications of their "apartness of objects".

On criticizing new historicism in literary theory, Harman goes against the politics of process philosophies, as he claims: "The strictly philosophical problem with this boundary-free holism is (that) relational ontology is incapable of thinking adequately about the concept of 'locality'" (Harman, 2012, 194). For Harman, the attention to the ongoing event fullness of process philosophies prevents them understanding objects that are under no current relation with other objects because this is what he means by locality: self-contained objects. Bennett uses Deleuze's notion of assemblage to challenge the idea that process philosophy necessarily represents a holism. She writes:

> [D]espite their robust attempts to conceptualize groupings, Deleuze and Guattari also manage to attend carefully to many specific objects, to horses, shoes, orchids, packs of wolves, wasps, priests, metals, etc. Indeed, I find nothing in their approach inconsistent with the object-oriented philosopher's claim that things harbor a differential between their inside and outside or an irreducible moment of (withdrawn-from-view) interiority.
>
> (Bennett, 2012, 227)

Once again, both perspectives have room for both analytic units, but they disagree on the ontological precedence and therefore the analytical priority.

Not surprisingly, given his explicit rejection of radical political movements, Harman links process philosophies to an illusion of liberation and claims that the commonly made connection between stability and oppression should be revised. In his words,

> [T]his is one of the most deeply rooted intellectual biases of our time. In the current landscape, the notion of autonomous substances seems to evoke a world of stagnant subjugation, while the dynamism of relational and materialist ontologies seems to open up a vast panorama of political and intellectual breakthrough.
>
> (Harman, 2012, 192)

For Bennett, the political dimension of the processes–objects debate goes beyond the liberating or restrictive character of each of them and bets for the alternation of processes and objects as the focus of the analytic process, for these kind of attempts "do justice both to systems and things, to acknowledge the stubborn reality of individuation and the essentially distributive quality of their affectivity or capacity to produce effects, to remain philosophically and (especially) politically productive" (Bennett, 2012, 228). Obviously Bennett's idea that we can alternate the analytic unit is of huge relevance for this book, and we will get back to it in the politics section. For now, let me give one more example of the confrontation between process-based theories and OOO. This should be the rejection of OOO toward the explicitly feminist side of new materialism.

In her article "Girls Welcome!", Michael O'Rouke (2011) offers a detailed account of the debates among some OOO theorists and some feminist/queer theorists; such encounters mostly happen in the blogosphere (the main trench of OOOs) and some conferences. The history is as could be expected, with OOO's authors being condescending and patronizing all the way through. The underlying reason for such a disencounter, Rebekah Sheldon (2015) explains, has nothing to do with feminism focusing on human identity politics and OOO being more ontologically focused; it is rather a difference regarding the understanding of the implications of knowledge production. Sheldon notes, "For object-oriented ontology, epistemology is epiphenomenal, a second order representation whose range of effects is limited to human knowers. For feminist new materialism, by contrast, epistemology is an agent with direct material consequences" (Sheldon, 2015, 196). In direct line with this idea, Katherine Behar (2016) has proposed an object-oriented feminism (OOF), aiming to infiltrate OOO with three important feminist commitments: politics, erotics, and ethics, filling an important absence in OOO that is nothing but the echo of the this male-centered spirit of continental philosophy (Kolozova and Joy, 2016). Sheldon's insight about the difference of the understanding of epistemology is of great relevance, as I concur that on prioritizing ontology, OOO forgets that epistemologies exist in the world as real objects – with sensual qualities – and therefore have causal relations that should be a priority for social sciences. This epistemological difference sets the base for a political one, for a theory that prioritizes ontology over epistemology, and that therefore denies epistemology as an ontological object, also neglecting the role of the author behind the theory and especially the fact that personal politics are framing such a theory. The real difference between OOO and process-based theories is not an ontological one; it is rather a political one, or at least it is the difference that carries the main consequences for the production of social theory.

My purpose in showing a little bit of this theoretical confrontation is not to contribute to this solution or to side with any of them. My leanings are quite clear in favor of theories based on process philosophy, which is due more to their political commitments than to their philosophical foundations. If I present this discussion, it is to make a point outside of the box: This discussion doesn't make sense for social theory. It doesn't help, as it is, to carry on with our agendas. Or, to put it simply, as they are currently used and explain, processes and objects do exactly the same. Both perspectives represent ontologically centered possibilities to account for change and stability. The challenge then would be to take strategic advantage of using the best of their resources to carry on with the agenda of social theory.

The socio-historic specificity and descriptive quality of social theory make irrelevant the philosophical distinction between processes and objects. In the world we live in, things stay and things continue; things change and have relations; those relations change, empower bodies, diminish others, alter capacities, or remain astonishingly forever quiet. If OOO can account for all those processes, great – thank you, guys. If process philosophies reach to the same result, terrific – thank you, too. But at the end of the day, it is the task of social theorist to account for the specificities of context using (or not) these philosophical models to produce theory that helps improve the conditions we live under. Furthermore, the distinction between processes and objects and the whole debate about which one should be at the center of philosophical, and for that matter theoretical, concerns should also be irrelevant for philosophy itself; isn't a flat ontology one that does not privilege a form of existence upon others? Shouldn't all forms of existence be worthy of theoretical treatment regardless their dynamism, or stability, or perceptibility, or thinkability, its humanity or lack thereof, its organic or inanimate status, or even more, the extent to which it participates in human practices in the form of a system, process, relation, or object, event, or other entity? But how should we do this? How can we alternate processes and objects toward a nonhuman understanding of human practices? And if they do more or less the same, why should we combine them? Why don't we take only one? My response to this is the third word mentioned at the beginning of this section – practices.

Practices

What makes what a body does more relevant than what a body is or vice versa? Such a question can't escape the interrogation of whose bodies we are talking about. What kind of relations are we interested in and why? Priority of processes or objects should not respond to an ontological concern but to a political one. In that sense, the politics of this book are closer to the politics of relational theories because my concern in exploring the social world is to better understand the conditions we live under so we can improve them. And to do so, it's still priority to look at who is doing what to whom, what the effect is of such action, what conditions empower or restrain the capacities of bodies, and to what end. To be clear, what are we doing? To who? What for? How? These are relational questions. However, if we look closely to the way these relations occur, we will witness the emergence of objects mediating or otherwise participating of such relations. This is what I have naturally come to conceptualize of practice.

There has been a historical interest in the theorization of practice in social theory, from the seminal works of Pierre Bourdieu (1990, 2005) or Anthony Giddens (1979, 1984) to the so-called practice turn in sociology (Schatzki et al., 2001), including the more recent interest of Wetherell (2012, 2015) and the deeply related notion of habit, like in the special issue on habit in *Body & Society* (Bennett et al., 2013). The idea of practice as an analytic unit has been coming back and forth, helping create theories, movements, and authors with different proposals of what a practice is and what it does. Practice is productive, a matrix of the production of subjects, objects, and situations that help explain the relations between us and the world; Bourdieu knew it a long time ago when he explained that practices are: "[t]hese discrete, self-sufficient units owe their immediate transparency not only to the schemes that are realized in them but also to the situation apprehended through these schemes in a practical relationship" (Bourdieu, 1990, 87). For Bourdieu practice cannot be understood as purely automatic, but neither can it be fully explained by free will.

For him, they are simultaneously "automatic and impersonal, significant without intending to signify, ordinary practices lend themselves to an understanding no less automatic and impersonal: the picking up of the objective intention they express in no way implies 'reactivation' of the 'lived' intention of the agent who performs them" (2005, 80). This variation in the degree of consciousness involved in the practice is what makes them great units to develop a non-correlationist approach.

Schatzki et al. (2001) describes practices as "embodied, materially mediated arrays of human activity centrally organized round shared practical understanding" (2). In his understanding of practices, it is the human body that allows us to see the connections between the subjects and the social manifolds, thus the practice is always materially mediated. This materiality involved in human practice is not always necessarily a human materiality; it could refer to objects, substances, things, and so on. Therefore, Shatzki also recognizes the role of the nonhuman as agencies that participate in the practice but also emerge out of them. Although this idea of practice displaces the human mind as the central phenomenon to analyze, Shatzki also recognized that practice is the main condition of possibility to mind constitution, for knowledge and understanding are first practical and then cognitive and symbolic. In a similar vein, Reckwitz (2002) suggests that practice involves a specific disposition of the body, a degree of conscious activity, and objects or things. Practice is an *affective* human affair; therefore, it takes a moving body/mind composition to exist, like a body sweating because it is hot, then picking up a fan and waving to mitigate the heat, and yet producing more heat in doing so. Practice involves things, animated or inanimate, organic or not, like the dishes we clean or the cookies we eat from a plate, or the fly that flies around our cookies. Therefore, practice implies the understanding of the relation between humans and *nonhumans*. Last, such relations involve some degree of ontological transformation of all the agencies participating on it; the fact that a practice is materially mediated means that the transformations emerging out of it are not only symbolic, or structural, or institutional, but they are *material* transformations. For example, you walk for two hours every day, and as a result you lose some weight. Practice is then necessarily a matter of concern for new materialism.

Here I understand practice as a matrix of activity that triggers process in different scales of reality and simultaneously animates aesthetic dimensions of reality, so the objects within them can relate through their sensual qualities. Practice contains human action and some meaning carried there but also activates biological process at the organic and molecular levels. When practice is carried out, repeatedly, it produces habits that eventually make cultures. At the same time practices change our bodies, and new objects emerge from this changing: other smells, other textures, other patterns of temperature. Practices constitute the aesthetic correlates of our cultures; we make the objects that solidify and represent our practices, like gluten-free bread or hipster outfits. Practices also work to promote and expand certain ways of being in the world by using some objects to pass indescribable experiences that can be communicated only as lived, felt experiences, like different forms of art or cooking. If practice is productive of rearrangements at different scales and aesthetic dimensions, the human component is rather a pretext, a starting point to explore beyond it, and certainly a point to return to, but only after having gone far away. My understanding of practice relies on the productive capacity of practice while exploring what else is produced in a practice beyond the human affair or beyond what we can empirically observe about it.

Within affect studies, Margaret Wetherell has recently proposed a turn to practice as a sort of antidote to what she recognizes as "wrong turns" in the study of affect. The problem that she recognizes is basically the lack of concreteness of affect studies and the "celebration of the uncanny" that comes with it. To fix this, Wetherell understands practice as

> a way of conceptualizing social action as constantly in motion while yet recognizing too that the past, and what has been done before, constrains the present and the future. Practice is both a noun and a verb. It is an activity and for participants (and social analysts) it is also an established reference point and site of repetition.
>
> (Wetherell, 2012, 23)

Although I wholeheartedly agree with the dynamism and temporal concerns of this understanding of practice, Wetherell's solution, when applied to the analysis of social practices, relays heavily in human meaning making and the discursive expression of such a practice (see Wetherell, 2012, Chapter 4; Wetherell, 2013, 2015). It is fair to recognize that this is a refreshing discursive approach to affective practices, but the whole point of my approach is to offer a nonhuman-centered approach to human affairs. Therefore, my interest in practice is only as a point of access to the worlds that it creates. I don't want to look at practices for practices' sake or for the human meaning making of it; neither do I want to study practices only for what practices do to bodies as human organic systems. Practice for me is not the end of the trajectory but rather the starting point. Unlike Wetherell, for me, affect, or practices for that matter, can't be studied as purely empirical. If I choose "practice" as an analytical unit, it is not to rely on the empirical qualities of a practice; it is rather to have a starting point from which to open up to speculations. When Wetherell claims "with affective practice rather than circulating emotion as the unit of analysis, relationality would re-appear" (2015, 160), she is only talking about a relationality that is empirically accessible for her. This is not exclusively Wetherell's fault, for no discipline is harder to escape correlationism than for hers (and mine): psychology. No other discipline is more colonized and therefore prone to privilege (certain) human access to reality by means of rationality. Like other psychologists, she wants an empirical access to create a method, to deliver rational accounts of a life that goes way beyond our access to it and the knowledge that could be produced from there. That is certainly not my use of the notion of practice. For Wetherell, "[p]ractice certainly pushes more towards habit than the uncanny" (Wetherell, 2012, 23). And that is not what I want. I claim the exact opposite – that practices open up the uncanny to our partial understanding, which is necessary if we are to go beyond correlationist approaches to human affairs.

Within affect studies "habit" has been a concern due to its automatic nature and therefore its relation to nonconscious processes; Blackman (2013), Massumi (2015b), and Hui Kyong Chun (2017) have developed great insight in that regard. For Wendy Hui Kyong Chun (2017), this automatization of habit can be explained in terms of receptivity to the external world being internally transformed into "unreflective spontaneity, beneath personality and consciousness" (9). Such spontaneity occurs in a way that escapes conscious control or awareness. There is certainly a co-productive relationship between habits and practice, for habits produce practices with some degree of conscious awareness by virtue of body training; and practices, if repeated, might eventually produce habits regardless of the degree of consciousness with which they were enacted in the first place. We need to distinguish between habit and practice precisely because practice refers to events of behavior, things we do, and it might be a one-time-thing as a part of a larger process. Habits are different; they refer to historical practice that contract specifics within the self. The habit allows the body to be the way it is, to come to existence as an object with history and continuity. But as Deleuze explains, such a different and particular form of existence needs to be achieved by means of repetition. This means that habits need to be made. Before that, we don't yet have the propensities and readiness that come with habit; the subject is still to be made. We have, however, an entire world of processes and objects being related (or not), with sensual qualities causing effects on other objects.

Habit also has the implications of being a pure human thing; a practice, however, could be any behavior acted out by any organic entity, even if it is not human, even, and especially if, such a creature has a different cognitive and conscious capacities or a whole different system of awareness, like carnivorous plants or a platypus. Therefore, practice is more about what an organism activates in the world, regardless of the current degree of consciousness. Massumi explains this by asserting,

> When I act, I am more of a catalyst for the reactivation of those forces than a direct commander or autonomous willer. That's always the case, to one degree or another. Our freedom doesn't consist in making a choice or decision that comes only out of our own subjectivity – in other words, out of nowhere. Our freedom is how we play out implications in the field, what events we succeed in catalyzing in it that bring out the latent singularity of the situation, how we inflect for novel emergences.
>
> (Massumi, 2015b, 158)

Although the notion of habit will be eventually useful throughout the book, I want to take practice as the main analytic unit due to its eventual and open nature.

Before I explain my model to take practice as the analytic unit to track process and objects within our digesting reality, I want to point out some crucial qualities of the concept of practice in this book:

- **Practice is affective.** Not only because practice is the pure manifestation of a process of affecting and being affected, as we do something with some things, we do something to them, we let them do something to us, affect us. But also, the communicative capacities of the body and the transmission of affect are actualized through practices as nonconscious components of the affective process.
- **Practice is materially mediated**. When we do things, we bring our bodies into specific registers, we change the way the body exists either for some seconds, or forever, or slowly and non-stopping. The main way to maintain ourselves in the world is by processes of transubstantiation, like eating and drinking, or medicine taking, or just breathing air. There is a material perpetual interpenetration. Doing something means materially changing the being; practice is ontological transformation.

- **Practice involves nonhumans**. Everything we do, even two naked human bodies making love to each other, involves a relation with nonhuman agencies: a drop of sweat on the forehead, a pattern of temperature, an orgasm, the air we breathe, the cigarette afterward. Beyond sex, everyday human practices involve a variety of objects of different nature, more or less organic, like fruit or chairs; more or less animated, like birds or software; more or less material, like a poem or a snowflake.
- **Practice creates subjectivity.** Practices involve practical understanding, material predisposition, the emergence of a sensible base for the development of subjectivity. The ways in which we understand the world rely on material predispositions that allow different forms of subjectivity; they bring certain tendencies or propensities for bodies to think in specific ways. This is important because an understanding of practice as the base for the emergence of subjectivity is the key to the development of a nonhuman-centered approach to human consciousness.

If the debate of objects versus process, as profound as it is, it is only superficially relevant for social sciences, and if practice is for now an alternative to study human affairs as an affective, material, nonhuman matrix toward a non-anthropocentric understanding of subjectivity, there is still the question of how to do it.

Multilayered model

Only when we do things does reality becomes reachable, thinkable, even to some extent empirical. It is activity, or what here I call practice, that unfolds the multiple changes and stabilities within which our human life is embedded. To better digest the complexity of this reality, this model proposes to understand reality as made of multiple scales and multiple dimensions. These scales and dimensions are crisscrossed by virtue of the processes and objects contained on them.

A scale of the reality is a plane of existence that can be known and/or manipulated by human consciousness to a specific and variable degree. This is due to the fact that agencies participating in each plane are ontologically diverse, and so are the systems of relations emerging from them. A scale of the reality is an analytical unit that helps describe systems of relations or, as we will call them in the rest of the book, processes that are triggered by human practice or intersecting with them and affecting the potential of bodies, including the conscious capacities of those bodies.

An aesthetic dimension is a transversal hub of activity that crosses through different scales of the reality. An aesthetic dimension is constituted of different objects, and these objects are defined by their capacity to modify affective experience for humans in their encounters with other humans and nonhumans. An aesthetic dimension is an analytical unit that helps us understand the finitude of the entities that partake in human life or, as we will call them in the rest of the book, objects, that participate in the interchange of properties involved in human practices affecting the potential of bodies to feel and transmit feelings. To be clear, processes belong to different scales. Objects belong to different aesthetic dimensions.

We need a model that combines processes and objects for a couple of different reasons. First, we need process because without a processual understanding of reality, we would lack the historically situated political dimension of reality. The price of tremendous loss for the understanding of human affairs would be nothing less than ignoring questions related to social structures emerging in historical processes where specific conditions have been created for different genders, races, classes, degree of disability and other categories used to "other" individuals and populations and send them to the boundaries of social life or even beyond them. Second, we need objects because without introducing the object as analytical unit, we would lack the concreteness of every piece of reality we relate to, and ironically, we would lack attention to the process triggered by the interchange of qualities among objects. Furthermore, reality, as we experience it, comprises entities with defined boundaries, a beginning and an end, and the existence of such objects is expressed in aesthetic events that are consubstantial to reality and need to be addressed to understand social

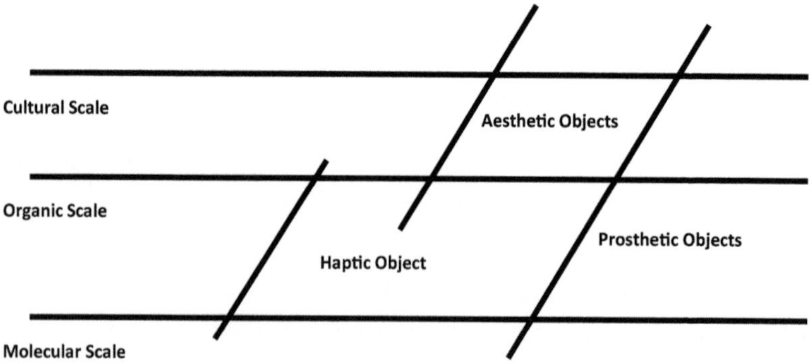

Figure 0.1 Multilayered model

life. So, relying only on the study of process misses the limited access that entities have to each other, and this is crucial to understand how processes belonging to different scales of the reality connect to each other through aesthetic events (see Figure 0.1).

Scales of the reality

The idea of "scales of the reality" is inspired in a processual understanding of activity within which we can identify process incorporating agencies of different nature and, therefore, having an ontological diversity. The idea of a multiscalar reality is by no means new; it's actually inspired in diverse affect and new materialists' scholars like Luciana Parisi, John Protevi, and Mark Hansen.[4] The distinction of three scales of the reality is based on the difference in degree of access and manipulation that human consciousness has on the process ongoing at each scale. This degree of access and manipulation variates due to the ontological diversity of the elements interacting at each scale. The distinction of three scales of the reality allows us to look at how human agency variates on the different systems of relations produced and manifested within these planes of activity.

The *molecular scale* belongs to the infra-empirical level. It is made of objects and processes that seem too small to be accessed by humans' systems of perception. I'm using the term "molecular" here as a metaphor to refer to all processes and objects operating below human perception, regardless the fact that they are smaller or bigger than a molecule. This includes atoms, neurons, cells, and other complex structures from which the material world we know is made of. The objects and processes in the molecular scale might have a relationship with human consciousness, but such a relation is rather indirect or technologically mediated. For that reason, to explore molecular events, I rely on the description of insights coming from different fields of science, like molecular biology, quantum physics, and neurosciences because these fields of science rely on technology to give us access to the molecular realm. The relation between conscious and molecular events is indirect when molecular process are affected as a consequence of human conscious activity, for example, as a result of a human deciding to change by the way they eat. It is indirect because we decide to eat differently not to alter a molecular process in an specific way. This is a consequence that escapes our conscious control. The relation between molecular scale and human consciousness is technologically mediated when we modify molecular (neuronal, quantum, cellular) activity by means of technology or biotechnology, for example, when we design or intake a drug, or a technologically mediated procedure to alter molecular events in a desired direction like laser surgery or chemotherapy. But ultimately our will has to be translated to a material event that triggers the desired process. In short, molecules don't behave differently only by virtue of our conscious power or will; they behave differently either as a consequence of another event, like drinking too much alcohol, or they behave differently because we force them through technological mediation, like in biomedicine. Humans can't ask molecules to do something; they have to make them do it. The molecular scale of reality can be partially known and always through technological mediation. It can be partially manipulated and always through technological mediation. It can't be manipulated directly by human consciousness.

The *organic scale* belongs to the empirical and phenomenological realm. It is made of processes and objects as we know them and of the experiences we live by. I'm using the term "organic" to refer to the fact that in this scale we recognize our bodies as full working organisms, even when this is only one side of the reality of our bodies. In the organic scale, we humans live in our bodies. In the organic scale we relate to objects as finite entities in relation with other bodies. We wear shoes, sit on chairs, witness romance between giraffes, eat an apple, surprise at a fight between a carnivorous plant and a bee, and watch the autumn dry trees out. The relationship between the events at the organic scale and our human consciousness is of partial control and manipulation; therefore, disciplines such as organic biology, psychology, or ethology have a lot to offer to help in understanding this partial manipulation of reality. We can perceive to some extent objects and processes within the limited range of our perceptual apparatus. This is important because this flaw-full perceptual system is the base upon which modern science has defined the empirical qualities required to legitimate knowledge. In the organic scale, we can consciously manipulate our relations with other objects or our involvement in a given process, like when you decide if you are going to have another beer or when you decide to go to watch a movie. Even if the organic event emerges out of someone else's will, we still can consciously respond, like when you decide to express your madness at somebody who has eaten your food. In this scale, we can also create certain objects, like when we write a book or prepare a salad. In short, humans can access, manipulate, and create processes and objects to some extent in the organic scale of the reality. But such access is restricted by our cognitive capacities, mainly perception, and is restricted as well by other organisms' willpower and conscious activity.

The *cultural scale* belongs to the symbolic and structural correlate of reality. It is made of cultural process of the institutions and subsystems that shape public life. I'm using the term "cultural" to preserve the sense that the expressions of public life are context and time specific. Even global policies or institutions are embedded in the particularities of the locations where they express their existence. The cultural scale of the reality includes objects less tangible than those in the organic scales. The objects in the cultural scale are, for example, institutions, such as the Catholic Church in Mexico City or the University of East London, and subsystems of public life, such as public health system in New York or the public transport system in Buenos Aires. The cultural scale of reality also includes the process that dynamize the institutions and subsystems, like the policies, rules, laws, and implicit understandings of specific aspects of reality that are shared in a given culture. This is what other social science has described as the symbolic aspects of culture or the discursive formations that emerge out of institutions and subsystems; therefore, disciplines such as sociology, cultural studies, or social psychology have a great deal to offer in this scale. The processes and objects occurring within the cultural scale of reality can be partially accessed by human conscious, for example, when you hear that a modification on migration flows has been approved or when you are notified that prices on electricity are going up this year. As informed as you can be, the manipulation of the process in the cultural scale of the reality cannot be done by an individual consciousness. It takes a system to change a system or at least the organized sum of individual wills, which is already a system. Human agency needs to be mediated by a system to manipulate processes at the cultural scale of reality. To be clear, you don't ask capitalism to disappear; you get organized with your community to slowly make changes. In short, humans can partially know, understand, and be aware of the process going on at the cultural scale, but humans cannot manipulate cultural processes by virtue of will or conscious power; such power requires to be mediated by a system. Cultural scale or reality can be perceived by human consciousness but can't be manipulated by one single human consciousness.

Aesthetic dimensions of reality

The idea of an "aesthetic dimension of reality" is the one that allows me to incorporate the insights offered by OOO. Here I understand an aesthetic dimension of reality as a plane of aesthetic causality where objects emerge, interact, and give up relations. As Morton (2013b) suggests, if the modification of an object is to appear in the world, this can only happen in the way such an object is perceived by another object; this means the only thing that can be modified in an object are the sensual qualities through which it relates to other objects. Thus, aesthetics is the plane of causality, OOO claims. In that sense I distinguish three aesthetic dimensions because I recognize three planes of activity where objects with different compositions are affected; based on Harman's (2011a) quadruple object theory, I identify the following objects within the practices I look into in this book: 1) a type of real objects with sensual qualities that I call haptic objects; 2) a second type of object appearing mostly as a sensual object with sensual qualities that I call aesthetic objects; and 3) a third type, which is a sensual object with real qualities that I call prosthetic objects. Harman's real object with real qualities does not appear in my analysis because it doesn't belong to the plane of relations involved in human practices. For OOO, objects are clusters of objects; every object contains the quadrupleness of sensual and real objects and sensual and real qualities. The typology of object that I offer is not different from this. If I feature each of them as being mainly sensual, or mainly real with mainly sensual or real qualities, this is not an ontological claim. It is rather an analytic strategy to point to the profile of these objects when participating in human practices. Thus, in theory, my objects are functions of objects rather than ontological objects; so are Harman's.

Thus, the distinction of my three aesthetic dimensions of reality is based on the ontological differences among objects that participate in human practices. Such objects possess a different degree of relatedness with human consciousness, and they engage in relations that carry aesthetic consequences altering for the potential of bodies (human and otherwise) to affect and be affected. Crucial among the activity in these aesthetic planes is the fact that objects redirect operating systems of relatedness in other objects. This means objects change the way other objects generally relate to them or to others. For the human being, this basically means that objects redirect regimes of perception and make things appear in the world (for us) as they relate. The second important feature of these objects is that in their relations, they create other objects whose existence is crucial for humans because they work as the backdrop for subjectivity production.

A typology of the objects emerging from such aesthetic dimensions allows us to understand what objects emerge out of objects' relations and how the capacities of bodies are modified in and by these objects. Analyzing objects allows us to see how the connection between processes that are ontologically diverse (the scales of the reality) are not processes themselves; the relations among different scales of reality are better expressed and explained by objects as understood in OOO because they emerge as new entities whose nature exceeds their relations. Thinking objects, like OOO proposes, also helps us speculate where their real qualities are left – what exactly is withdrawn. What part of the object is not participating in the encounter with the human? If objects encounter each other, when we talk about encounters between humans and other objects, the part of the other object that is not participating in the encounter has potentially to appear in other encounters, for other objects, even if it's not for us and only stays in the domain of nonhuman relations. Some of the objects in my typology are objects that appear for the human body or even within the human body; others are totally a nonhuman affair. These objects are the following:

Haptic objects appear mediating the molecular and cultural scales. They emerge out of events in the molecular scale that reach a form of existence in the organic one. I call them haptic objects because they only exist for human bodies as they enter into direct contact with human body through one of the systems of our sensorium. Haptic objects emerge from another body but need to enter our own body to be perceived. Haptic objects can be perceived but can't be manipulated by human consciousness, only after being filtered by the body. This means that they are objects emerging from human bodies but whose production is not consciously elaborated by the subject; however, the subject has access to perceive some of the sensual qualities of such an object. For example, the texture of someone's skin can be touched by themselves or another subject; however, the owner of the skin has no power to modify, by virtue of consciousness, the texture of their skin. It's the result of a molecular process, and as we have argued before, molecular processes can't be consciously manipulated, but an intervention could be achieved by technological mediation. For example, after applying hydrating creams for a long period of time, skin texture doesn't change out of people's will; we have to make it change. Skin texture, as a haptic object, relates through its qualities and redirects our regime of perception. That is how haptic objects connect molecular and organic scales; they are the result of activity in the former, but they are perceived by organic mechanisms in the latter. The reason it is so important to include haptic objects in our model is because they are a crucial part in human practices. They represent the ontological concreteness of the sensual dimension of human practices. Smells, textures, colors, patterns of temperature, sounds, patterns of bodies' balance, flavors, thickness of hair, greasiness of nails, light in someone's eyes, body shapes, pain, stability, awareness of the body, thirstiness, hungriness, caresses, and orgasms are all haptic objects connecting molecular and organic scales while bringing aesthetic dynamism to the practice.

Although all objects contain real and sensual objects and real and sensual qualities, what characterizes haptic objects is that they appear to us primarily as real objects with sensual qualities. Their sensual qualities are so invasive that they literally enter our bodies, and that creates the desire of knowing or feeling more about them, the call to what we cannot access, the real object. Harman (2011a) defines this as the allure, the effect of the real object with sensual qualities, the desire of knowing that there is something else to such object and yet you will never access it. Containing the quadruple cluster, in relation to human practices, haptic objects are mostly real objects with sensual qualities.

Aesthetic objects are mediating the organic scale and the cultural scale. I call them aesthetic objects because these are the objects that we can physically recognize in the organic scale of reality, and therefore their aesthetic qualities are of immediate access to humans. Unlike haptic objects, aesthetic objects don't need to enter our bodies to be perceived or felt; their properties act at a distance, so their presence has effects before we notice. These objects can be consciously produced by human beings, like sunglasses or apple pie, and can also be consciously perceived by humans, like when we see the decorations in a vegan restaurant or when we eat an apple before it goes into a pie. It is important to point out here that whereas both objects, haptic and aesthetic, involve the sensorium to be perceived, haptic objects emanate from human bodies, and aesthetic objects don't emerge out of human bodies but out of the conscious process of human creation, like a piece of art or a lamb born out of farm insemination. Aesthetic objects have an independent life from human beings even if they were created by us. They relate to other objects, and in these relations, they produce new complex objects whose effects escape or bypass human conscious. These new atmosphere-like objects emerge out of the relations among aesthetic objects, and they create a sensibility that is a backdrop for ideology, a sort of propensity in the bodies that welcome some subjectivity better than others. For example, to create a restaurant, we can design or make decisions about furniture or dishes, decorate a place, design illumination, make music, and so on, but these objects will interact to create an atmosphere whose effect will bypass the consciousness of the human being involved in such atmosphere. They will feel relaxed, or excited, or warmed up.

Although all objects contain the quadruple cluster that Harman explains, my aesthetic objects appear to humans as sensual objects and relate to them through sensual qualities – sensual objects with sensual qualities. According to Harman, when a sensual object overwhelmingly throws sensual qualities to a perceiver, there is a moment in which the whole sensual object appears like a "unified kernel dangling its qualities like marionettes" (Harman, 2011a, 103). He suggests the term *confrontation* to describe this fully sensual experience in which we can recognize the whole object and all its sensual qualities. Where there is a wholeness integrated in the experience of the perceiver, this is the main feature of a sensual object with sensual qualities, as is the case for what I'm calling here aesthetic objects.

Prosthetic objects connect all three scales of reality from molecular to cultural and passing through organic. I'm calling them prosthetic objects for two reasons. First, they expand the capacities of bodies, allowing them to affect bodies beyond the natural reachability of the body, and second, they are able to communicate and even reproduce certain body configurations within other bodies. Prosthetic objects not only extend a body's qualities and capacities; they emulate the state of bodies within other bodies, like a body duplication. Thus, the prosthetic object is capable of taking qualities, even if not stable ones, from one scale of reality and translate them into the next one; in that sense there is a cross-scalar property of some objects. If prosthetic objects also have a sensual quality, then haptic objects and aesthetic objects might have prosthetic effects. But prosthetic objects are also capable of taking states of qualities of a body and communicating to other bodies within the same scale; in that sense the prosthetic objects are also cross-dimensional. Prosthetic objects connect our three scales of reality and our three aesthetic dimensions (as long as they could be functions of haptic and aesthetic objects). A plant prosthesis translates molecular processes into flavors that can be perceived by humans; a human prosthesis writes a poem about that flavor that produces emotions in other bodies; a poem prosthesis then creates cultural moments and aesthetic tendencies. Prosthesis is a feather in the hat warning you about the wind or a car that let you feel the road in a nonhuman way. Prosthesis is language expressing emotions and triggering empathy in another body. It is the first large object that I could find to scratch my back precisely on the unreachable spots with precisely the force needed. Prosthetic objects increase the capacities of bodies and expand the aesthetic effects to scales or dimensions previously unaffected.

Prosthetic objects are sensual objects with real qualities. They appear evident and self-explanatory. We seem to have direct access; however, what we see is a wholeness that is not yet giving away the nature of what it can do. Harman has suggested that sensual objects with real qualities seem to unify in the surface qualities that have withdrawn. There is then a permanent tension contained in this kind of object, the tension of what they seem to be and the feeling that there is more to them, but we won't know what. For Harman, only *theory* can "reverse-engineer" this fusion between sensual objects and real qualities that seems to always have already happened. Through a book, the main prosthetic object explored is a written one, sometimes in the form of poems, sometimes of experimental writing. They are by no means the only prosthetic objects present in human practices, but as we will see in Chapter 5, the nature of this research has only drunk from these waters.

This multilayered model is meant to be an understanding of reality that goes beyond human sovereignty to consciously act and represent the world. To do so this model includes scales of reality and aesthetic dimensions with objects that cannot be manipulated by human will power and that, despite human representation, their activity remains independent. The scales of reality and the processes within them are defined by the degree of agency that they allow to human consciousness, and the aesthetic dimensions and the objects within them are defined by the ways they increase or decrease affective capacity for human bodies and experiences. Perhaps Table 1.1 helps us understand these relations. In the first

Table 1.1 Relation to human consciousness with reference to affective capacity

Scales and objects	*Relation to human consciousness*	*Affective capacity*
Molecular scale	• Can't be directly known or manipulated • Could be partially known and manipulated trough technological mediation	• Affect itself via matter
Organic scale	• Can be partially known and manipulated through conscious process	• Affect becomes emotion via language
Cultural scale	• Can be partially known • Can't be manipulated by individual consciousness	• Affect can be elicited via manipulation of assemblage
Haptic object	• Can be perceived • Can't be manipulated by conscious	• Affect can be intensified via conscious perception
Aesthetic object	• Can be created and manipulated by conscious	• Affect can be intensified by bypassing consciousness
Prosthetic object	• Can be partially known • Emerging from humans, can be created and manipulated by consciousness	• Increases capacity to affect other bodies • Increases capacity to be affected by other bodies

column we see the relation to human consciousness of each of our six units (three scales and three objects), and in the second column we see some of the affective consequences that are crucial to understand the role of each unit in human practice.

Organization of the book

To account for the dynamism among our three scales of reality and three kinds of objects, each chapter presents and theorizes a segment of the model by choosing one practice and one object or process: a practice such as eating a taco, or drinking a glass or wine, and a process or object at stake within such practice, like the production of heat or the emergence of desire. Chapter 1, "Tacos and Heat", establishes the three scales of reality, molecular, organic, and cultural. Chapter 2, "Veganism and Politics", uses the same three scales but complements the model by adding the analysis of the objects that connect the three scales: haptic and aesthetic. Chapter 3, "Chocolate and Desire", focuses on the relation between molecular and organic scales, particularly in the way consciousness is involved to produce desire. Chapter 4, "Wine and Time", continues to focus on the relation molecular-organic, and the role of consciousness, but this time on its relation to matter and the effects on human perception of time. It also introduces the prosthetic object as a methodological resource. Chapter 5, "Mezcal and Knowledge", explores the relation between organic and cultural scales, particularly in the epistemological implications of nonhuman knowledge emerging from the interchange of properties of the human body and the role of prosthetic objects to explore such knowledge. The chapters are organized in the following fashion:

Chapter 1 creates a speculative approach to the process of thermoception. Based on Whitehead's concept of prehensions and his analysis by divisions, this chapter explores the production of heat in the context of eating street tacos at night in Mexico City. Thermoception here works as a process involving the events of production of heat within three different scales of the reality: molecular, organic, and cultural. The chapter borrows contributions from molecular biology to explain how human thermoceptors interact with capsaicin molecule, then we rely on social psychology to account for organic events of heat through rites of interaction, and finally the chapter explores the history of emotions to claim that in a Mexican context there is a special kind of anxiety, called "ansias", which is an emotion constituted by heat within the practice of eating street tacos. The general aim of the chapter is to introduce the three scales of reality that will remain throughout the book and offer a way to analyze and speculate about a multiscalar reality.

Chapter 2 takes the case of veganism to theorize the emergence of the political dimension of life as a dimension constituted by process and objects that crosses our three scales of reality. The analysis of the political dimension of veganism requires the incorporation as well of two objects: haptic and aesthetic. The chapter aims to reconsider the way of theorizing politics in social sciences by moving the focus from relations of power, inequality, or dominance to the analysis of emergent patterns of organization of matter and emergent aesthetic reorientations of regimes of perception. As the description of politics of veganism goes in this chapter, I argue that in the molecular scale, veganism raises the politics of "slowing down" protein synthesis; in the organic scale it triggers the politics of "tracking" vegan places, people, and even the vegan self; and the cultural scale entails the politics of "compassion" that ties practice and identity through institutions. Similarly, the haptic objects reorient the sensual qualities of objects emerging from the organism, such as skin and smell, and the aesthetic objects, that is, the objects associated to vegan culture, like products or ornaments, create the vegan atmosphere as the backdrop of vegan sensibility.

Chapter 3 takes the process of production of desire for chocolate – or feeling a chocolate craving – to explore the relation between the molecular and organic scales. Particular attention is paid to the conscious capacities of human organisms and their deliberative power as capacities that help us rethink the sovereign status of individuals. The chapter is informed by mix of neuroscientific discourses, theories of neuroplasticity, and Deleuze and Guattari's notion of assemblage as well as the distinction between molar and molecular strata of organization. The purpose of the chapter is to account for the cross-scalar trajectories of social and organic forces involved in the process of production of desire, such as environmental arrangement, organic memories, and so on. The chapter ends by proposing a political use of neuroplastic resources focused on the aesthetics of experiences to modify the process of production of desire for food toward a better management of food consumption.

Chapter 4 continues the theorizing of the relation between molecular and organic scales, but unlike the previous chapter, in this one I address a different aspect of the molar-organic relation, namely, the effects of material activity of objects in human consciousness and particularly in our perception of time. To do so, I have chosen the scenario of two persons sharing a bottle of red wine to explore the role of matter in the perception of time. I rely on Bergsonian philosophy and his concept of duration as a philosophical framework to integrate material-temporal events in the understanding of human perception. This chapter is additionally informed by Barad's concept of diffraction as a resource to speculate about wine's properties and potential events being diffracted in time as well as Stern's concept of attunement to account for the rhythmic interchange of bodies within the organic scale. To do all this, the chapter incorporates the resource of experimental writing, as a prosthetic object, that works as a means for speculation on the tempo-material relation between molecular and organic scales.

Chapter 5 explores the aesthetic dimension of drinking mezcal through the creation of poetry as prosthetic objects to rethink the possibilities of nonhuman knowledge and its epistemological consequences for the production of human knowledge. The chapter is based on a project of poetry production based on different varieties of agave (the plant mezcal is made of), each of which was written out of a "mezcal meeting" between me and somebody else. Those poems were used for the back labels of the mezcal bottles and to theorize what it would mean for epistemology to acknowledge the existence of knowledge in nonhuman agents, such as plants or drinks made of those plants. The chapter gives relevance to the role of poetry as a methodological resource to speculate about nonhuman knowledge and the implications for epistemology. Whereas the chapter focuses on poetry as prosthetic objects, it also acknowledges that poetry and knowledge are objects emerging in between organic and cultural scales.

Finally, I will close the book with a brief section addressing the way in which my multilayered model contributes to the study of human subjectivity by creating what I call a nonhuman understanding of human practices. In the same final section, I explain the politics of this project to make a two-sided movement: first, pointing out the politics of philosophical traditions mixed up in my model, process philosophies, and OOO to make the corresponding critique, and then, explaining the role of politics according to my approach.

Notes

1 As I will explain throughout the book, Graham Harman (2016) has published a book that aims to show how social scientists should use OOO to do social sciences; his idea and ways of doing it seem to me extremely far from what social sciences should do. In a similar way, in the last twenty years there have been hundreds of contributions explaining how we should use process philosophies in social

sciences. Although I'm more sympathetic to these approaches, most of them also miss the point of creating theoretical contributions to the understanding of human lives.

2 Elsewhere, (Lara, 2015) I have explained that the way fields like affect studies have taken on process philosophies is rather a conceptual fragmentation of such philosophical approaches, where one or two concepts are isolated without a deep integration of the whole philosophical frame.

3 Whitehead is a little different because in his philosophy there is a unit to name something that has already become and that dwells in a state that is not processual at the present moment; this is his idea of concrescence.

4 Luciana Parisi, *Abstract Sex. Philosophy, Bio-Technology and the Mutation of Desire* (London: Continuum, 2004). Parisi explained the stratification of abstract sex, defining three scales with different logics in terms of sexual reproduction and also the production of sexual desire; she addressed biodigital, biocultural, and biophysical "layers", defining how each work with different information transfer modes, rules of organization, and different modalities of sex and also how each line corresponds with specific dates in the evolution of organisms and evolution of science. Each layer corresponds to a different practice of sex in Parisi's theory: turbo sex for biodigital strata, aquatic sex for biocultural, and microbial sex for biophysical. Important to this contribution is that Parisi pointed out the fact that sex is expressed in different layers of the reality through different modalities, meaning sex is a process socialized beyond and above the human organisms, and the full comprehension of sex requires this sort of account, including different strata or what we call here scales. John Protevi, *Political Affect, Connecting the Social and the Somatic* (Minneapolis: University of Minnesota Press, 2009). Protevi proposed a perspective called political physiology "to indicate that subjectivity is sometimes bypassed in favor of a direct linkage of the social and the somatic" (xi). Protevi develops "three basic concepts – bodies politic, political cognition, and political affect – to examine the interlocking of the social and the somatic. The concept of bodies politic is meant to capture the emergent – that is, the embodied/embedded/extended – character of subjectivity or, in other words, the way the production, bypassing, and surpassing of subjectivity is found in the interactions of somatic and social systems. In bodies politic, the inherent relations of freedom and constraint, of individual and group, of subordinations and hierarchy, make these systems amenable to political analysis; the regulation of material flows performed by these systems makes them objects of physiological study; and the triggering of qualitative different feelings by those material flows, as well as the subtle negotiations of dynamic coupling of social emotions, makes them the object of psychological study. These networks of bodies politic are knitted together by the interlocking of processes that link the patterns, thresholds, and triggers of the behavior of the component bodies to the patterns, thresholds, and triggers of the behavior of the emergent superordinate (and sometimes transversal) bodies. His analysis then "posits three compositional scales of bodies politic – personal, group, and civic – as well as three temporal scales – short – term, mid-term, and long-term" (xii). Mark Hansen, *Feed Forward. On the Future of Twenty-First-Century Media* (Chicago, IL: The University of Chicago Press, 2015). In the same multiscalar spirit, Mark Hansen has recently proposed a post-phenomenological phenomenology, inspired in the philosophy of Alfred N. Whitehead, as an effort to go back to the study of subjectivity and

human experience through the study of what he calls twenty-first century media. Hansen engages with these new technological sensory devices whose data processing act outside the registers of our perception or conscious activity but yet come back to it to amplify our relation with the world; in his perspective this sort of environmental non-perceptual sensibility constitutes "our multi-scaled, disparate agency in the world" (183).

1 Tacos and heat

In this first chapter I'm going to introduce the three scales of reality and show how they work when related to an everyday process, the production of heat. To explain the multiscalar nature of heat, I will rely on an everyday practice in Mexico City, eating street tacos. But why are heat and temperature a good starting point?

Experiences related to eating are intimately linked with temperature in a lot of ways, for example, the molecular process through which we "burn" the calories by metabolic combustion of sugar in a process is known as metabolism (Ong, 2012). We also use fire to cook, and this has been suggested to be the condition of possibility for the modification of human bodies and thus for the evolution of human kind (Whrangham, 2010). We organize the agricultural production of food in relation with climate change and the variable temperature of the seasons (Schellnhuber et al., 2006). In the aesthetic and affective domains, pleasure and enjoyment of food have also been associated with food's temperature, like the pleasure of having hot drinks to counteract the cold environment (Lee et al., 2003). In general, the perception of the flavor of food changes in relation with temperature (Englen, 2012). Eating provides a clear example of a broad spectrum in which temperature is a relevant agency to be explained for its potential to modify the affective capacities of human and nonhuman bodies.

Temperature has recently been brought to affect studies by Vannini and Taggart (2014a, 2014b) under the label of thermoception. However, current approaches to thermoception focus on the conscious experience of production and regulation of heat and do not consider those events of production of heat that bypass consciousness and yet partake in the thermoception process and the human experience of heat. In this chapter, I draw on Whitehead's philosophy to propose a speculative account of thermoception capable of integrating different events of production of heat through an analysis of the "division" of prehensions, in which each prehension is an event of production of heat needed to explain thermoception. To do so, I analyze the production of heat in the experience of eating tacos[1] at street *taquerias* of Mexico City. When eating, different temperatures connect, and new ones are created: the food's temperature, the temperature of the human body, that of the atmosphere, and the new ones emerging from the interactions among them. However, eating tacos in the streets of Mexico City is a particularly illustrative case for the thermal processes involved on eating practices because, as we will see, the thermal dynamism involved in eating street tacos involves elements and processes passing by, bypassing and surpassing conscious awareness that has hitherto been the focus of the study of thermoception. Of particular interest in this chapter is the way prehensions of heat modify the capacity of the body to feel heat in the molecular, organic, and cultural scales of activity, and how the concatenation of the production of heat among such scales is at stake in the production of subjectivity, as well as the production of what I call heat emotions – anxiety in particular.

Recent approaches to thermoception address it as a process of active involvement with the modification of ambient and body temperature. Vannini and Taggart suggest that "this involvement is an expression of the capacity of bodies to be affected by and affect ordinary sensations such as thermoception – the bodily feeling of temperature." Such an involvement in that processes, the authors go on, "is transformative" of the ambient and therefore they conceptualize it as "catalytic" (2014a, 65). Vannini and Taggart developed this insight by studying the production of heat in off-grid houses, in which heating the space demands dwellers be physically involved. As they explain "the functioning of off-gridders' hot energy home systems heavily depend on a process of education of their attention" (2014a, 79). So thermoception here is something that you learn to regulate. The production of heat is understood as a dynamic process, "an interface" requiring bodily involvement through a "hub of activities" oriented to modulate the world; it is "a nexus of intersecting practices" and should be understood as "participation" in the transformation of temperature rather than passive "perception" (2014a, 66). That is to say, Vannini and Taggart's thermoception is full of will; it is a conscious activity of physical involvement for the regulation of temperature.

Following Vannini and Taggart's ethnographic approach, Allen-Collinson and Owton (2015) also subscribe to the importance of studying the possibility of controlling and being aware of thermoception. They conduct autoethnographic and autophenomenographic research to address what they call "lived heat" through "warming up and thermoregulation"

(2015, 3) as experienced and accounted by women receiving physical training in distance running and boxing. Phenomenological approaches to different cultures of heat also have been conducted using "participatory observation" to explore the way one intentionally warms up and cools down before and after dancing (Potter, 2008). Phenomenological sociology has been used to address the sensory dimension of heat on athletes practicing distance running and scuba diving (Allen-Collison and Hockey, 2010). Even Ong's elegant proposal on the aesthetics of heat in architectural design highlights "our ability to control heat [as] the basis for subsequent development of human culture, technology and society" (2012, 10, brackets mine). More or less explicitly these approaches share in common the claim for a consciously driven management of bodily participation in the thermoception process. It is then rather surprising to find that all the aforementioned studies found inspiration in Classen's (1993) explanation of Tzotzil's cosmology of heat in Mexico. Although they all evoke Classen's Tzotzil to argue the relevance of studying heat, they fail on recognizing that a cosmology is a version of the universe including different scales of organization and plenty of agency – that is, of the capacity to affect – and all of which are connected to each other: from the hot sun to the chili peppers and the spiritual heat of the *chaman* providing thermal order to space and time. In Tzotzil cosmology, thermoception is not a process mediated – let alone regulated – by human conscious. It refers to the flux of heat across the universe in which many forms of heat agencies bypass consciousness and yet participate in the modification of the capacities of the human body (affect) and the production of human (nonconscious) subjectivity that are important to fully understand the affective experience of heat. By citing Classen's Tzotzil cosmogony of heat, current approaches to thermoception are rushing away from such a cosmological understanding; they rather stay close to approaches that allow them to operationalize methodologically the study of heat. So they stay with another favorite, Ingold, as he allows them to approach heat as an "involved activity, in the specific relational context of their practical engagement with their surroundings" (2011, 10), and thus heat is again under the domain of human conscious activity as the epicenter of these "surroundings" from where such an "engagement" is managed.

Before I move to explain how I will expand thermoception out of the conscious domain, it is worthy to note that such an obsession for conscious regulation has its origin in the understanding of the "human body as organism".[2] This idea, Clough (2008) has argued, is embedded in scientific discourses from late nineteenth century, especially in thermodynamic laws[3] and the belief of the organic tendency to homeostatic equilibrium. These scientific discourses were the condition of possibility for emergence of the so-called disciplinary society. Disciplinary science, Parisi and Terranova explain

> was intrigued by the movements of solids, objects falling through spaces, but also by the constancy of energy and its irreversible processes marked by accumulation and discharge, The disciplined body is the thermodynamic organism, the hierarchical organizations of organs, bounded within a self, crossed by currents of energy tending towards entropy and death.
>
> (Parisi and Terranova, 2000)

The human body, thus understood as an organism operating upon thermodynamic laws, was thought to work strictly to reach homeostatic equilibrium. To be able to do "work" and preserve equilibrium (and participate then in the economic system of production and reproduction), the human body needed to be understood in this strata of organization in which it is an organic whole body. Such an organism, Parisi and Terranova explain "is determined by consciousness and is the place where consciousness operates. It is the most visible and molar aspect of the human body" (Parisi and Terranova, 2000, np). The body as organism provided as well a "bio-physical pattern through which the organism came to be conceived as *homeostatic*" (Parisi and Terranova, 2000, np); it is, with a fixed consciousness concerned with the regulation of the temperature. The organism is then "defined autopoietically as open to energy but informationally closed to the environment, thus engendering its own boundary conditions" (Clough, 2008, 2).

Studies on thermoception focus on the production of heat as a "capacity to do work" (Vannini and Taggart, 2014) or a sort of conscious regulation of bodily heat (Potter, 2008; Allen-Collinson and Owton, 2015) or controllable thermal conditions of the ambient (Ong, 2012) because they all share the idea of a body as an organism looking for homeostatic thermal equilibrium. However, if there is any legacy to affect studies, it is precisely the consideration of new advances in science and technology, particularly those in relation to new scales of organization of matter with their new logics that define control society. Late twentieth-century advances in quantum physics and molecular biology generated understanding of levels of organization of life and matter working outside of thermodynamic laws and under far-from-equilibrium conditions (see Prigogine and Stengers, 1984; Clough, 2004). As a consequence affect studies have been able to generate new understandings of the body such as the "turbulent body" (Parisi and Terranova, 2000) or the "bio-mediated body" (Clough, 2008). These proposals share in common the critique of the autopoietic body on the basis of techoscientific contributions that understand the body as open to information. In addition, further advances in new materialism (Bennett, 2010; Barad, 2014) have made important contributions to acknowledging the agency of matter and in consequence have provided a base to rethink human subjectivity in relation to material interactions free of conscious deliberation.

What is clear for both affect studies and new materialism is that material relations from small scales of activity (molecular and quantum) do not work under the same logic as autopoietic organisms; molecules do not follow thermodynamic laws, nor do they pursue any kind of homeostasis. As Parisi and Terranova explain it,

> It is with the emergence of complexity theory that disequilibrium becomes a principle of reality. Rather than a return to the primary cause according to a linear development which regulates the origins of life, the perception of a body through complexity theory and molecular biology involves a break with its physiology. In these terms, a body no longer corresponds to the fleshy representation or phenomenon of the human subject, but rather is opened up to particles, waves and attractors, which constitute it as far from equilibrium system.
>
> (Parisi and Terranova, 2000)

Once science has made its contributions, accounting for human subjectivity also requires a different philosophical frame that can include the logics of molecular organization rather than neglect them as a "pure science" that may not relate to human subjectivity. Alfred N. Whitehead refers to this possibility of exclusion as "the bifurcation of nature", and his whole speculative project was fully devoted to overcoming such a trend that is so present in Western anthropocentrism (Shaviro, 2014a). Whitehead's philosophy is particularly helpful here, if not yet to get close to Tzotzil's cosmology of heat, at least to propose a speculative account of thermoception able to expand the explanation of human experience of heat beyond its conscious affairs. Whitehead's radical ecology accounts for "causal efficacy" among organisms of different grades of complexity without giving privilege to perception, which "is confined to 'high-grade organisms' that are 'relatively few' in the universe as a whole. On the other hand, causal efficacy is universal; it plays a larger role in our own experience than we tend to realize, and it can be attributed 'even to organisms of the lowest grade'" (Shaviro, 2011, 281).

For Whitehead, the universe is full of events that he called "actual occasions" or "actual entities" organized in different levels of complexity or "societies". Those actual occasions come to be by virtue of their relations with other actual occasions through a process of multiple prehensions. In Whitehead's philosophy prehensions are "concrete facts of relatedness" and in general "each process of appropriation of a particular element" (Whitehead, 1985, 219). Shaviro describes Whiteheadian prehensions as including both "causal relation and perceptual ones – and [Whitehead] makes no fundamental distinction between them. . . . Whitehead's key term prehension can be defined as any process – causal, perceptual, or of another nature entirely – in which an entity grasp, registers the presence of, responds to, or is affected by, another entity" (Shaviro, 2011, 281, brackets mine). Prehensions as an act of response have also been articulated by Clough as preconscious and pre-individual, "a kind of knowing, an affective knowing, prior to individuation and consciousness" (Clough, 2012) Then, prehensions are not a human-exclusive property; they are rather affective enactments with vector qualities, connecting what is here with what is there (see also Parisi, 2004). Regardless of its nature, any actual occasion can be divided into different prehensions participating in its becoming. As Whitehead explains, "[E]ach actual entity is analyzable in an indefinite number of ways. In some modes of analysis, the component elements are more abstract than in other modes of analysis. This mode of analysis will be termed the 'division' of the actual entity in question . . . that mode of analysis which exhibits the most concrete elements in the nature of actual entities" (Whitehead, 1985, 19). What is most relevant of this kind of division analysis of prehensions is the idea that each prehension reproduces the qualities of the actual entity and then inherits particular qualities proper of its own eventness.

In what follows in this chapter, I will embrace this idea of the analysis of division of different kinds of prehensions to articulate my speculative account of thermoception. Division analysis of prehensions is the analytic device I use to advance beyond the current accounts of thermoception centered in organic-conscious-homeostatic activity. To do so, I will describe the particularities and relations of three different levels of prehension that actively participate in the thermal experience of eating tacos in Mexico City: molecular, organic, and cultural. Each of those prehensions is, in its own way, an event of production of heat that concatenate to each other to give shape to the subjective experience of thermoception. Of particular importance in this account is the Whiteheadian assumption that subjectivity is not a exclusively human – organic and conscious – capacity; instead he would claim a "processual subjectivism" in which subjectivity "not only ranges across all scales of matter but . . . emerges from the bottom up" (Hansen, 2015, 10). Thus, each of my events of production of heat entails its own quota of subjectivity that will be inherited all the way up to the human subjective experience of heat, sometimes bypassing conscious register, though. This is crucial because it is the main reason to claim that an organic-conscious-homeostatic-centered account of thermoception is not enough to explain the human experience of heat. In fact the concerns of these approaches inevitably take their authors to a methodological problem, that of being anchored in a traditional idea of empiricism incapable of accounting for events at stake in the human experience that are not analyzable by their methodological resources whether "ethnographic approaches to the experience of heat" (Vannini and Taggart, 2014, 62), "empirical phenomenological sociology" (Allen-Collinson and Owton, 2015, 2), "participant experience" (Potter, 2008, 446), or the "poetical" description of architecture as "the orchestration of heat through energy, climate, and habitation" (Ong, 2012, 7). To solve that problem, we may appeal to a speculative empiricism that as Whitehead has explained, has as its purpose "the endeavor to frame a coherent, logical, necessary system of general ideas in terms of which every element of our experience can be interpreted" (Whitehead, 1985, 11).

Organic prehensions

I want to start where all accounts of thermoception have started: the organic scale of activity. The event of eating appears to happen at first on this scale among defined organisms, including human bodies, food, and also nonhuman bodies as objects and devices with important participation in our eating scenario: the *taqueria*. As it is easy to guess, a place in which hot food is prepared requires a source of heat, more precisely a source of fire; we will also call them "fire devices." In Mexico City streets you can find at least two different kinds of *taquerias*: the "makeshift street stalls" and restaurants whose seating spills onto the sidewalk or that are open to the street so you can see the "kitchen" when you pass by. The type, style, and use of fire devices will depend on the kind of tacos offered in each place; for example, griddles are used for charred beef and sizzling pork or tacos *de carne asada*; rotating vertical spits for tacos with hunks of marinated pork with pineapple called tacos *al pastor*; or hotplates for the slow-cooked pork we call *carnitas*. We can take those three fire devices as representative; it is even common to find them all together because a *taqueria* usually offers a variety of tacos that requires them all. But fire sources vary almost as much as tacos fillings; we can even find fire devices like holes in the ground with burning stones inside covered with maguey leaves, in which sheep meat is slowly cooked. Eccentric as it sounds, you can eat sheep tacos cooked this way in the streets of Mexico City;[4] we call it *barbacoa*.

Whatever they are using as a source of fire for the cooking, the fire device and the heat emerging from it will usually share a feature: They are outdoors. Even when we are talking of a "restaurant", they are open to the weather; the walls of buildings are actually huge blinds that can open, turning it into an outdoor place. In addition, the fire device is commonly located nearest as possible to the street; sometimes they are even taken outside and onto the sidewalk. This has a simple purpose: to facilitate the traveling smells, so people passing by in the street can easily feel a craving for tacos. Smells are not a minor detail. Brennan (2004) strongly documented the importance of smell in the transmission of affect by pheromones; she wrote "pheromones (are) molecules that can be airborne and that communicate chemical information – signal and produce reactions by unnoticeable odor in many hormonal interactions" (2004, 9). So, for Brennan, social interaction modifies the biology of bodies and is thus crucial for the experience of affect. In the context of *taquerias*, these pheromones and smells emerge directly from the activity of the fire device; smells are the first salient consequence from the activity of the cooking fire device. As the mediator between the *taqueria* and the city, smells are part of the thermoception process; they are essential and consubstantial in the emergent temperature.

Heat smells through the *taqueria*. This smelling heat stands also as the geographical boundary of the territory, the scope of the *taqueria* is defined by the scope of the emergent heat, so in these scenarios there are not physical boundaries defining the territory but thermal ones. You can observe different kinds of *taquerias*, different fire devices, and special and geographical distributions in Figure 1.1, 1.2, and 1.3. These photographs were taken in the streets of Mexico City by Mexican artist Sofia Cruz.

The encounters between heat emanating from fire devices, city weather, and smells engage in thermal dynamics that fit what Vannini and Taggart, following Stewart (2011), refer to as an atmospheric attunement, "an affective force that manifests itself in involvement in the lifeworld and in its transformation" (2014a, 66). In Whiteheadian terms, the prehensions we can find in this organic scale of activity are those associated with this atmospheric attunement, like air temperature responding to the heat emanating from the fire devices and of course the human bodies "feeling" such a fixed temperature, which for Whitehead might be better described

Figure 1.1 Rotating vertical spit as the fire device in Taqueria Nacho

Figure 1.2 Makeshift taco street stalls outside the subway, night and eaters included

as a positive prehension. Notwithstanding, the human body at this stage fits what Vannini and Taggart called a "cool" energy coming from on-grid heating, in which the human bodies are less involved in the production of heat. In this case this "on-grid" heat is given for the fire devices in the *taqueria*, and the human bodies appear to be quite passive on the reception of such heat;[5] they are not working, running, boxing, or dancing but quietly sitting or standing. In the organic level of prehension, the human organisms are not yet actively participating in the production of heat, not in a relevant fashion. However, as soon as you start eating, the body becomes another source of heat and thus more active in the process of thermoception. There is one organic element here with its own agency to trigger heat and modify the chained process of thermoception: it is capsaicin, the molecular component in the soul of chili, which is an essential component for a taco.

Molecular prehension

Whoever tells you that the salsa on a taco is optional is a tourist. The fact that you have to add it yourself does not mean that it is optional. It is not yet part of the taco because you are supposed to be able to choose the type you prefer. It is rare that one would not have at least a little; in Mexico even children add a few drops to their tacos. It is possible to find sliced marinated habanero peppers (sometimes with pineapple) or roasted red or green peppers with salt; those are possibilities, but what you will doubtless find is a couple of bowls with two salsas – one green, the other red. Those colors are actually broad categories in and of themselves that contain a massive variety of chilies, ways of preparation, and ingredients, from garlic to cilantro, to local worms like *jumiles*, to alcoholic beverages like *pulque*.

The burning sensation that occurs from the spicy intake is due to capsaicin, which is the main pungent component in "hot" chili peppers. Nobody remains unaffected after biting into a chili. As Chef Zahie Tellez (2011) explains, it is a very intelligent plant: "[W]hen you bite a chili it bites you back." More than a simple pun, the "biting back" of the chili is an expression of the agency of the molecule, the stimulation capsaicin elicits over the heat and pain receptors of the skin, which causes a more intense blood flow and a strong burning sensation in the mouth. The brain, cheated, believes that the body temperature is rising dangerously, and implements the necessary mechanisms to alleviate it, including sweating and dilation of blood vessels, causing the flush. This is the sensation of being on fire, of sweating bullets, which one experiences when eating chili. Your body responds to the heat source and becomes another source of heat and more active in the process of thermoception. Of course, the body is a source of heat by itself, and eating modifies our internal temperature even without capsaicin, just by increasing the system's activity; but what is at stake here is a particular molecular interaction that triggers larger thermal consequences.

Molecular biologist Caterina and her colleagues (1999) have explained that capsaicin elicits a sensation of burning pain by selectively activating sensory neurons that convey information about noxious stimuli to the central nervous system.[6] Capsaicin receptors are usually activated by increases in temperature in noxious ranges, suggesting that they function as transducers of painful thermal stimuli (Caterina et al., 1997). A great deal is now known about the molecular basis of sensory perception, especially in the visual, olfactory, and gustatory systems in which cell surface proteins that detect changes in our physical or chemical environment have been identified.[7] These molecules endow sensory neurons with specialized receptive properties, thereby determining how we perceive the world around us. As Caterina and Julius explain in relation to pain, it "is also a sensory modality in which specialized primary afferent neurons, called nociceptors, detect noxious stimuli" (2001, 248). Nociceptors are remarkable and unusual sensory cells because they respond "to a broad range of physical (e.g., heat, cold, and pressure) and chemical (e.g., acid, irritants, and inflammatory mediators) stimuli, but do so only at stimulus intensities capable of causing tissue damage" (Caterina and Julius, 2001, 487). Caterina and Julius (2001; see also Jordt and Julius, 2002) have provided insights into the activation of primary afferent nociceptors and have revealed the ability of some nociceptors to act in an efferent capacity by stimulating inflammation, smooth muscle contraction, or secretion in target tissues. Those bodily responses are the new events of production of heat coming from the prehension among the molecules of capsaicin by the nociceptors in the nervous system, a new pattern of the body that elicits heat production by virtue of its activity on molecular prehensions.

Capsaicin elicits burning sensations through the activation of a heat-gated ion channel called VR1 on sensory nerve endings, which is likely to contribute to the detection of painful thermal stimuli (Caterina et al., 1997). VR1 seems to be our internal thermal regulator that informs us about noxious heat levels; it is also activated by heat (>43°C). Notwithstanding, in the context of the *taqueria*, high thermal levels come from the intake of chili that activates the nociceptors, and the entire arsenal against possible pain in the body is a heat-evoked response to the ongoing molecular prehension. But there is no noxious heat level in the body. It is just the chili's capsaicin activating this alarm, and so the supposed "appropriate protective responses" become aesthetic elements of the experience of eating spicy tacos. It is a display of agency by one of the molecular components at play in the eating experience of tacos. When you experience capsaicin you start to sweat, cheeks become red, you start salivating, you are breathing with your mouth open, and your blood has changed the rhythm of its flux. You are literally hotter and emanating heat. We do not feel the molecular prehension, but we experience it through its effects. Visceral capsaicin-sensitive afferent neurons are involved in both reflex autonomic responses to visceral stimuli (e.g., changes in blood flow, heart rate, or respiratory rate) and the conscious perception of visceral discomfort (Ness and Gebhart, 1990). So it has been proposed that "these cells represent 'warm' receptors involved in the regulation of core body temperature" (Caterina and Julius, 2001, 492). Many proteins, including receptors and channels, show alterations in their structure or activity as a function of temperature, but "VR1 has thermal response characteristics that make it especially interesting in the context of nociception. Most notably, VR1 is gated by heat but only when ambient temperatures exceed <43°C, a threshold matching that of heat-evoked pain responses" (Caterina and Julius, 2001, 500).

With the molecular prehension between capsaicin and nociceptors, VR1 modifies the temperature of the entire human body, and thus it becomes another source of heat, ready to be re-prehended by the already attuned atmosphere described in the previous section. If the temperature of the body changes, the pattern of relations of the atmosphere changes too. At this point the human body experiences the catalytic property of involvement suggested by Vannini and Taggart (2014a) as "something that has transformative power of an assemblage within which it operates", but unlike their account, here the body does not become a source of heat by virtue of conscious management of physical involvement but as result of a molecular prehension that consciousness does not register until the moment further effects appear in the organic scale (flushing, sweating, etc.). Thus, thermoception involves positive prehensions in which the atmosphere intakes the body as part of its own enchained process; but these bodies are themselves the result of another level of prehension, the molecular one.

Whitehead explains that

> a molecule is a historic route of actual occasions; and such a route is an 'event'. Now the motion of the molecules is nothing other than the differences between the successive occasions of its life history

> in respect to the extensive quanta form which they arise; and the changes in the molecule are the consequential differences in the actual occasions.
>
> (Whitehead, 1985, 80)

Then, as VR1 and its nociceptors experience capsaicin again and again, the pain threshold is moved; the organic body changes the way it feels. It is not rare that Mexicans can (and like to) intake amounts of salsa that may not be enjoyable for other organisms. Molecular prehensions modify the way the organic body experiences heat; the organism is culturalized without conscious participation here. Consciousness, when appearing in the process of thermoception, has already inherited a history of molecular encounters of prehensions. So far, we have two different events of production of heat from two different scales of prehension in our thermoceptional tracking: the atmospheric attunement from the organic scale as a result of encounters among fire devices, weather, and smells and the VR1 turning on the fire alarm because of the encounter between nociceptors and capsaicin. Now that everything is hot, we should explain the interactions among these different sources of heat.

Cultural prehension

The cultural prehension is not located in a specific body, like fire devices or nociceptors; it is rather the historically rooted spatio-temporal process of interaction between those bodies. In the cultural scale of prehension is culture itself that responds to the production of heat; Whitehead refers to this kind of process as "conceptual prehensions" in which eternal objects are involved. Explaining the production of street tacos will help us understand the cultural practice involved in the interactions among different sources of heat. We can recognize three steps in the production of street tacos; each of which plays an important role in the final configuration on the taco and involves variations in the participation of different agents: they get closer, touch each other, talk, leave, get into each other, and so on.

In sidewalk and street open *taquerias*, the process is similar: there is always an already defined offer of tacos; they could offer fillings such as *suadero*,[8] sausage and mixed tacos, ribeye, and so on. Whatever the tacos are filled with, this has been decided long before you get there, and thus, in this moment, the level of participation of the eater in the taco's configuration is only in choosing among limited options. This is the first step; we can call it, "What is your taco?" After that, in the second step, the taco maker asks you if they should "add it all" to your taco; it usually means chopped onion and cilantro. So at this point you decide if it's going to be just onion, just cilantro, both, or neither. In this step of the process the configuration of the taco has turned into a sort of co-configuration. There is dialogue between the maker and the eater, all happening close to the fire device, because you have to be that close to indicate how much onion/cilantro and in fact to hear and be heard over the street noises. This second step could be called, "How is your taco?" The third step begins when the taco maker gives the tacos to the eater, and the eater goes away from the fire device to give the last nuances to the taco. Now the eater must finish the preparation. This moment is going to define things, like which salsa is added or whether to squeeze lime over the top. These two are the usual, but depending on the place, there may be other trimmings and complements available (some offer cooked potatoes, sliced vegetables, cucumbers, beans, etc.), contributing to this moment as the most playful and intimate in the process. You add to the taco what is about to be added to your body. This is the step in which the eater personalizes the taco. We can call it, "What do I add to my taco?"

In any step of the process, the order of the organic elements changes, from the moment the subject is caught in the taco atmosphere to the first bite, and those changes appear as a rite of reconfiguration of bodies where the body goes through a process of modification of temperature. Social psychologists Stenner and Moreno (2013) have addressed this processes of transition between two states as a liminal affective experience, where "having an experience" is understood as passing from a certain pattern of relations that is modified to come into a new pattern. In their words, liminality works "as the experience of being on, or crossing over, a threshold, then we begin to understand why affects and emotions are liminal phenomena of transition, and why liminal situations are affective and emotional" (2013, 242). Stenner and Moreno follow the broadly Whiteheadian proposition that affect is the transition between different orders or what mathematicians call a "vector." This idea, they go on, "would fit Whitehead's ontological definition of actual occasions of experience as events of transition from actuality to actuality" (2013, 238). The concept of liminality could even be extended into the ontological domain; as Szakolczai has pointed out, having an experience "means that once previous certainties are removed and one enters a delicate, uncertain, malleable state; something might happen to one that alters the very core of one's being" (2009, 148). Cultural practice as liminal experiences resonates with Whiteheadian process philosophy and helps us think through an ontology in which experience is fundamental to all forms of reality (Stenner and Moreno, 2013).

This liminal threshold is a cultural practice of interaction of our different events of production of heat in the *taqueria*; it is featured by prolonging close contact with the fire device(s) as well as with the other eater bodies (perhaps already producing heat) you have to share the space with – sometimes standing beside you, they ask you to reach the green salsa, to move so they can get another lime, and so on. The cultural rite of preparing a taco defines the way bodies engage with the process of thermoception; it determines the order of the events of production of heat. We start by becoming part of the atmosphere at the display in the *taqueria*, and this happens in a specific way: People leave the climate of the weather to enter into the microclimate of the *taqueria* – we get into its thermal territory – where the fire devices are already at play. We have to get close to the fire device, and this part of the rite catalyzes the attunement with temperature, but then we have to leave that source of heat, and afterward we are allowed to get in "touch" with the salsa and its capsaicin, even when we have been smelling it since the beginning. This process is important precisely because it gives the time and space for the atmospheric attunement of the organic prehensions before the molecular prehension by which the body is turned into another source of heat by eating salsa. The order of the events is not a minor detail; the experience of heat would be quite different if the internal heat emanated before or at the same time that we underwent atmospheric attunement. The specificity of the liminal cultural practice conveys its own quota of subjectivity that will be inherited to the whole experience. To this point, the role of atmospheric, molecular, and cultural prehensions in the affective experience still need to be prehended by the world of subjectivity; otherwise, thermoception cannot be completely accounted.

Anxiety: a heat emotion

Here is where all our former prehensions inherit their quotas of subjectivity to human experience. If, as I have claimed at the beginning of the chapter, the experience of heat when eating tacos is more than what consciously registers in the organic scale of activity, then we still need to understand how this thermoceptional process is prehended by a highly complex level of occasion; that is, the prehension of all these events of production of heat and their quotas of subjectivity by the domain of human subjectivity. Here it seems a good idea to appeal to human subjectivity by explaining signified affects or what most affect theorist would call emotions. The attention over thermoception brings us directly to one fundamental emotion associated in this particular context: anxiety. Anxiety is here an emotion made of heat. For this last level of prehensions, every previous prehension in the thermoception process has set a condition of possibility for anxiety. Such conditions of possibility may be expressed in the same scale of prehension, or in another one, or in all others; every event of the production of heat has a new and unique capacity for evoking emotions. Such an actual becoming through a novel production of togetherness or the coming together of multiple prehensions is what Whitehead called concrescence (Clough, 2012). This means that previous prehensions have set patterns prehended by human subjectivity.

Molecular prehension drops its quota in the organic scale, what is achieved from capsaicin activity a physiological anxiety. This anxiety is bio-chemically and molecularly anchored by the intake of spice; the prehension of capsaicin leads us to this physiological kind of anxiety, in which sweating, flushing, heat emanation, and an increase in salivation change the rhythm of the body, all physiological responses from the "cheated" brain shaping a bodily situation that the body feels it must escape from. The body feels like it's burning (but it is not). The anxiety there is an organic one, looking for thermal stability; the body wants to get away. This molecular prehension is read by the consciousness as a state to be solved, but being on fire is also a matter of pleasure; eater bodies do not suffer or do not dislike that suffering. To be on fire when eating is an anxiety that mixes pain and pleasure. After all, capsaicin in certain quantities is also associated with pleasure and arousal (Caterina and Julius, 2001). This particular form of anxiety-pain/pleasure pushes the body against the homeostatic equilibrium heralded by the conceptions of the body as an organism and founded in thermodynamic laws. Being on fire is the organic-physical condition of the possibility for anxiety. This organic anxiety matches and mixes with the cultural one; they have been together all along such that they can't be explained separately.

As all food does, eating a taco has historical and cultural implications. A record of affects and emotions have been historically attached to this practice as well as to the taco as a particular object mediating the practice; this record of historical affect is what Stearns and Stearns (1985) would call an emotionology. Here, the anxiety is rooted in the history of the country; it is pretty much a "cultural anxiety". Coveney (2000) has suggested that anxiety about food is usual in contexts of economic vulnerability and histories of precariousness, contexts in which the lack of food has been a regular part of the past. This makes sense for the Mexican context in which the necessity of prevention for times of precariousness is always present, especially at the time of eating. This feeling of perpetual economic vulnerability comes from the history of poverty caused by spanish colonization and is fed by a political context in which hopelessness is the main sentiment, at least for the working class. People eat like they are celebrating, but far from being a happy idea, what they are actually celebrating is the fact that they have food. We eat anxiously because an idea resonates in our minds, as my mother would say it: *Hoy podemos; mañana no sabemos* (today we can; tomorrow we can't tell)! We eat quickly, in certain haste, as if the precariousness were running after us, haunting us, ready to take away our food. This haste and quickly eating also produces heat. In a precarious context we eat as we live, with some anxiety, with some trepidation. It is not an anxiety about the present context; it is about the past. It is a historical relation with food featured by the anxiety of uncertainty. As we have described before, the fire devices and the atmospheric attunement set the thermal conditions of the *taqueria*. This warmth and cozy temperature evokes another intimate atmosphere related with this cultural anxiety: the warm family kitchens, the very contexts where we learn to relate to food through precariousness and anxiety. As Probyn (2009, 2012) suggested the eater body is a sensitized medium; it expresses relations among history, places, cultures, and different parts of the body.

In addition to organic and cultural anxiety, there is a third one: the anxiety of pleasure.[9] In this regard Mol (2013a) has signaled the trickiness of talk about pleasure in diet advising, where recognizing some food as pleasurable would turn it into a source of anxiety and more desire. As Coveney (2002) suggests the pleasures we drive from eating are also the sources of anxieties around eating. This anxiety attached to pleasure fits with the cultural prehension of the liminal ritual of eating tacos. A comfortable temperature and desirable smells are our first contacts with the atmosphere; the visual, olfactory, and thermal channels are all stimulated. This is the point in which desire begins. Waiting for the food has started, and until the first bite, this stimulation is not going to stop. So such a desire is projected into the future but still not satisfied; this not-yet-ness is the structure of anxiety itself, Ngai (2005) would suggest. From the moment the heat – with its molecules of smells – is prehended, we are caught in a sensation of unsatisfaction. In the cultural prehension the quota of subjectivity has form of desire, and desire is consubstantial to anxiety-pleasure/ pain.

All sources of heat, when being prehended by human subjectivity, or what Whitehead calls "eternal objects", help compose the particular anxiety of eating street tacos in Mexico. We even have a word for this particular performance of anxiety made of different heats; we call it *ansias*. When you feel *ansias* something is constantly burning you. It could be your history, your body, your atmosphere, your food, and so on. *Ansias* is the particular embodied anxiety invoked by not being able to escape – from heat in this case. Hence, the liminal rite of eating tacos (cultural prehension) provides the anxiety of the yet-not-satisfied desire. It amplifies and lengthens the anxiety, so until the moment you have your taco in your hands, the anxiety is unbridled. To the moment of the first bite, atmospheric attunement (organic prehension) has already evoked the historical anxiety, and capsaicin (molecular prehension) has already been read as a physical anxiety. To the first bite, anxiety is already driving the whole experience; yet it is not any anxiety, but *ansias* – this complex combination of different events of production of heat encountering each other and evoking pain, pleasure, desire, and fear of precariousness entangled in the way humans subjectively experience heat when eating tacos in Mexico City (see Figure 1.3).

Every event of production of heat is related in a different way with the prehension at the scale of human subjectivity – a different evocative component of anxiety in the form of *ansias* that is not isolable, but at least we can speculate possible trajectories of heat within the experience. This interrelatedness among different prehensions and its final prehension by human experience is what I imagine Whitehead had in mind when he proposed the idea of analysis of "division".

Figure 1.3 Jorge's thermoception, Jorge's ansias

From conscious control to multiscales

Vannini and Taggart propose an understanding of thermoception as a "hub of activities", "an interface", "a nexus of intersecting practices"; where I may agree with them, I propose that the analysis of such "activities" should also include those beyond the domain of "practices" understood as organic or cultural, so thermoception may be rather understood as a larger "hub" connecting a variety of events of production of heat from different strata of organization beyond organic-conscious activity. Thermoception then constitutes a complex process you may "interface" with, but it would require speculation about the relations among involved events of production of heat as well as about the quota of subjectivity that each event inherits to human experience. If we understand thermoception as I propose, then methodological procedures concentrated in the organic relations and conscious activity such as ethnography, participatory observation, and phenomenographic and autoethnographic accounts quickly show their limits.

We have to acknowledge the relevance of events of production of heat participating in the thermal activity and having an impact in human subjectivity that are not happening in the organic strata of organization and, more important, that are not happening under the same (thermodynamic) logic. If we are to understand thermoception as a "sensation" rather than a passive "perception", as Vannini and Taggart suggest, we ought to keep in mind the contributions developed by affect studies and take seriously the preference for process philosophies (Lara, 2015). I have offered a speculative account of thermoception able to bring together different events of production of heat operating in different scales of organization of reality, such as molecular, organic, and cultural. The notion of prehension has been particularly useful here as it provides an abstract way of grasping every event of production of heat without forcing them to fit under the same logic. Instead prehension and the analysis of division allows a focus on the relations among different events with different natures and speculation about the quota of subjectivity they inherit to human subjectivity, that is, the way they partake in human experience while not always in human consciousness.

As affect studies have made clear, human body and human consciousness are crossed by bodies and events that do not belong to the same strata of organization of the organic body, and that then are not regulated by thermodynamic laws, nor do they produce any kind of work to maintain homeostatic equilibrium. On the contrary, if we look at the molecular activity, we may find events of production of heat pushing the organism out of its equilibrium by inducing a pleasure/pain experience. We always want more salsa because pleasure is not always in equilibrium. We find also the cultural prehension having effects in the molecular domain, changing the way nociceptors register heat, and then also changing the way the organism produces heat. Liminal ritual is culturalizing molecular and organic activity. Most important, we can see how human subjectivity and particularly emotions are not just fed by conscious activity but by any kind of subjectivity produced in different kinds of prehensions. Mexican *ansias* experienced when we eat tacos in the street is a good example of a complex emotion in which different kinds of heat evoke diverse emotional components, all of them mediated by heat production. Hansen (2015) has proposed the term "post-phenomenological phenomenology" to describe his account of human experience not centered in conscious activity. His proposal also turns to Whitehead's speculative philosophy; as he explains, "[W]hatever account of experience one builds up on the basis of Whitehead's metaphysical scheme will have to be a theory of experience that not only does not begin by privileging human experience but that is, at a very deep level, neutral concerning the specific qualities of its 'subject'" (Hansen, 2015, 14).

Addressing thermoception through a Whiteheadian analysis of division of prehensions helps us understand that the human body is informed from different scales of activity, from the molecular to the organic, to the cultural, all the way up to human subjectivity. As Clough (2008) explains, recognizing the agency of matter and the lack of social elements in actual social processes offer the most suggestive contribution of affect studies. Yet connecting such material agencies with organisms and cultural practices requires speculative philosophy. As Whitehead pointed out, "[P]hysical experience is emotional feeling, felt in its relevance to a world beyond. . . . But the feeling is subjectively rooted in the immediacy of the present occasion: It is what the occasion feels for itself, as derived from the past and as merging into the future" (Whitehead, 1985, 163).

Even though this speculative account of thermoception has used as an example a particular context delimited by culture, I want to finish by suggesting that the relation among the prehensions recognized – molecular, organic, and cultural – could represent steady coordinates for further research conducted in relation with affective experience. But, in a more abstract way, I also have suggested that taking a process or chain of events (like thermoception) considered relevant within an experience, and analyzing by interfacing with the different events that concatenate within the process, offers us the possibility of tracking experience in a deep way, and this represents a general strategy to further advance empirical research within contemporary affect studies.

Notes

1 A taco is a Mexican delicacy composed by a rolled corn tortilla filled with anything you have, added with a touch of salsa. Among those three elements and possible complements, permutations are infinite, especially if you consider the richness of Mexican gastronomy and the fact that everything can be a taco filling.

2 See Lara and Encios (2014) "*Ciencia Teoría Social y Cuerpo en el Giro Afectivo: Esferas de Articulación*" for a review on how different encounters between social theories and science have encouraged different understandings of the body within affect studies and particularly how the idea of body as an organism has changed with new advances in molecular biology and biotechnology.

3 As Ong summarizes the laws of thermodynamics, "[T]he second law of thermodynamics states that objects of the same temperature are in thermal equilibrium. The first law can be expressed in many forms but is essentially a statement of the conservation of energy. The second law again describes energetics in terms of temperature – energy cannot flow from a lower temperature to the higher. As a result, the third law then concludes that minimum entropy is reached when thermal energy is totally dissipated. This occurs at a theoretical minimum of −273°C. The significance of these laws is that taken as a whole, the entire course and history of the universe is framed within a story about the expansion and dissipation of heat" (Ong, 2012, 8).

4 For a complete version of the history of tacos that also includes a broader spectrum of the Mexican varieties, can see "P Planet Taco: A Global History of Mexican Food" by Jeffrey M.-Pilchner (2012). It also includes an interesting tracking of the expansion of Mexican food around the world.

5 Note that this chapter is exclusively addressing the thermal experience of the human bodies eating (the eater-bodies) in the *taqueria*, but as you can appreciate in the pictures, those are not the only human bodies on the stage. The body of the taco maker, for example, has a different thermoceptional experience. They do work, move their bodies, and produce heat in more actively than Vannini and Taggart's bodies, and then they become a source of heat.

6 Among other things, interest in capsaicin in molecular biology has to do with the fact that this compound not only activates sensory neurons but also renders animals resistant to painful stimuli (Jancso et al., 1967). Since this discovery, capsaicin sensitivity has proven to be an extremely useful functional marker for a subset of neurons that are specialized to detect unpleasant or painful (noxious) stimuli.

7 In this chapter we are addressing heat in the molecular scale as a sensorial modality caused by touch: the touching of capsaicin and our nociceptors. It is important to mention that the study of heat includes the exploration of nontactile sensorial modalities, like variations on color, light, and its effect in thermal comfort; see Candas and Dufour (2005) for a good example of it.

8 *Suadero* is a thin cut of beef from the intermediate part of the cow between the belly and the leg; it is slowly cooked and marinated. *Suadero* is probably the most popular filling in Mexico City. Because the intake of *suadero* is extended all day, it could be breakfast, lunch, and of course dinner. For an explanation of regionalisms within Mexico regarding tacos, see García-Garza, 2010, 2011.

9 The anxiety attached to eating is not the same anxiety attached to the guilt and shame that has been broadly documented by affect theorists; see, for example, Brennan, 2004; Ngai, 2005 or Leys, 2007. This is a more complex anxiety, more similar to the anxiety attached to sex documented by affect theorists like Probyn (2000) and Berlant (2011).

2 Veganism and politics

After having introduced the three scales of reality in the tacos chapter, in this one we are going to incorporate two of the three objects of the model. To do that in this chapter, I propose a novel approach for the analysis of the political dimension of human life. My approach takes a practice in which the human body is the epicenter of activity and the analytic unit from which our understanding of "politics of life" can be expanded by a descriptive analysis combining processes and objects. I will take the practice of eating vegan, as a habit-producing practice that 1) reconfigures regimes of activity and relations in three different scales of reality and 2) creates objects that reorganize senso-perceptual human experience to redirect the politically charged production of subjectivity.

When we eat, a political dimension of life emerges. Here, I use the case of veganism to argue that focusing on eating as an everyday practice is a good starting point to expand our general understanding of the political dimension of life by developing a cross-scalar analysis of the politics of life, as a model centered on a habit-producing practice shaped by processes and objects. Analyses of the politics of food and eating developed in the field of food studies typically address relations of power among institutions participating in the distribution and production of food, the capacity of certain populations to access food, and the historical processes through which such conditions are created (Bentley, 2015). The terms "food security" (Castle et al., 2012) and "food justice" (Gottlieb and Joshi, 2010) are popular in this approach. Another common approach to the politics of eating comes from a wide socio-cultural tradition in food studies, often relying on ethnographic research that describes the practices, construction of identities, norms, and rites revolving around food and eating throughout different cultures (Miller and Deutsch, 2014). There is also an important body of literature regarding the relations of gender (McPhail et al., 2012), class (Gross and Grosenberger, 2010), and race

(Vardi, 2010) behind the aforementioned problems of distribution, production, and access. Scholars refer to these relations as "food cultures" or "food cultural politics" (see Watson and Caldwell, 2005). These traditions have contributed a great deal to understanding the political implications of the relation between food and societies as well as solidifying the field of food studies. Their focus of attention, however, sets the boundaries of their approaches. Research on the politics of eating have so far focused on the effect of relations of power mediated by institutions (a lá Foucault) and/or identities (a lá critical theory) and their subsequent effect upon the practice of eating. Both approaches are deeply committed to the idea of a sovereign subject who possesses freedom. Such freedom is simultaneously something that the subject is responsible to manage and the object of manipulation of institutions. The focus on institutional control and politics regarding identity categories represent a limit in the analysis of the political dimension of life; this is not an exclusive problem of food studies but a generalized tendency in social sciences and humanities.

Some years ago, Jedi Dean pointed out that "the state-centeredness of mainstream political theory results in a reductive dismissal of alternative forms of and sites of politics that treats them as pathologies rather that contestations" (2000, 9). As response to such a critique and loads of similar ones, in recent years, new materialism[1] and affect studies have contributed to our understanding of the politics of life in at least two ways: 1) by bringing attention to the agency of matter to rethink human political agency and 2) by theorizing the intentional or incidental manipulation of material intensities that instantiate affective states in human bodies. In light of new materialism, politics is thus understood in a broad sense "as an ongoing process of negotiating power relations . . . rather than as a merely formal constitutional, institutional, or normative edifice" (Coole and Frost, 2010, 18). With the agency of matter being reclaimed, we advance toward an understanding of human political agency as a "non-sovereign agency" (Krause, 2015). On its part, affect studies has prompted our attention to "preconscious" and "pre-individual" processes that do not take place at the scale of the conscious organism (Blackman and Venn, 2010; Lara et al., 2017). Contributions from this field have extended our understanding of the political by exploring emergent assemblages of material relations and the way this affects human bodies. As Massumi warns us, "[B]odies can be induced into, or attuned to, certain regions of tendency, futurity and potential, they can be induced into inhabiting the same affective environment" (Massumi, 2015b, 56–57).

For the most part, new materialism and affect studies share a commitment with process philosophies proposed by figures like Deleuze,

Bergson, Whitehead, or James (Lara, 2015). The way I will use this processual approach to understand the politics of relations is by identifying and describing the general logic of organization, the common hub or motif that gives qualities to such relations, to explain what kind of regulatory system is emerging at each scale of reality. Although these process philosophies have been a solid foundation for the refreshing of the political previously argued, I think our understating of the political dimension of life might benefit importantly form the inclusion of objects, as understood by Harman's OOO (2011a, 2016). Objects can be included as an analytical tool to theorize the way in which the aesthetic dimension of reality withholds relations of causality among objects that actively participate in the political dimension of life. Once processes reach stability, once they stop flowing, we can read them as objects, and as I will argue throughout the chapter, this allows us to include aesthetic events or object as part of the analysis of the politics of life. Panagia (2009) has explained that the organoleptic configuration of the body possesses a political potential as long as the reconfiguration of this sensorium modifies the senso-perceptual regimes for human experience. This reconfiguration of the sensorium is an aesthetic event with political potential that should be treated as an object, not as a relation of power or a processual immanence.[2] I will argue that if we introduce Harman's model of the quadruple object (2011a), some aesthetic events can be explained as objects produced by encounters among other objects and with the potential to redirect human subjectivity. This is what my proposal is adding, a concrete way to follow Jane Bennett's project "to make both 'objects' and 'relations' the periodic focus of theoretical attention" (2015, 228).

It follows that an analysis of the politics of life that focuses on the relations of power between institutions and/or identities is not broad enough if we are to develop a cross-scalar understanding of the political dimension of life. Even if we include materialities and other forces in the analysis of the relation of power, the focus remains in domination and control. This is precisely because those relations depend on a conscious human agency acting over either matter or subjects, yet in some scales of reality there is no conscious human activity determining the effects of the relations at stake. Even more, in some dimensions of political life – like the aesthetic ones – there is no such thing as "power relations", like negotiations to gain or lose agency. Instead, the political act in aesthetics consists of making manifest something that was not there, the reconfiguration of what is perceptible in our engagement with the world. Thus, for now, we might best think of the "political dimension of life" as a complex system of emerging regimes of activity and aesthetic reorientations of an object's perceptible qualities. It follows that this cross-scalar approach for the analysis of such political dimensions of life should be concerned with the identification and description of those regimes of activity and aesthetic reorientations.

Taking the example of veganism, I will account for the concatenation of the political regimes of activity at three scales of reality. First, the "molecular" scale functions with a politics of "slowing down" in relation to the speed of the synthesis of proteins due to the difference in amino-acid profiles between animal and vegetal proteins. Second, the "organic" scale of veganism is dynamized by a politics of "tracking" in which a process of self-identity and habit production affects the ways in which vegan organisms pursue places, products, communities, and the vegan self. Third, the "cultural" scale works under politics of "compassion", whereby a particular version of reverence for life works as the cornerstone of an institutional vegan ideology and motivates a vegan sense of responsibility. Mediating these three scales – molecular, organic, and cultural – are two aesthetic dimensions held by objects whose sensual qualities reorient the senso-perceptual domain of human experience. First, my favorite, haptic objects mediate the molecular and organic scales. Those are objects emanating from the human body holding sensual qualities that can't be controlled by the human mind. Haptic objects are not consciously produced but could be consciously perceived, for example, the smell, color, or texture of human skin. Haptic objects participate in the political dimension of life because they reorient the senso-perceptual domain in human experiences. Second, aesthetic objects mediate the organic and cultural scales. Those are objects surrounding and related to practice and have relations among them that provide new aesthetic objects. Aesthetic objects are created and put in place by human conscious agencies, but the effect of their relationships stick to humans at the preconscious, affective level, for example, the dishes, places, and products used in vegan culture and the atmosphere that emerges out of them. Aesthetic objects participate in the political dimension of life because, through their relations, they create the material basis for the sense making or subjective understanding of life.

Thus, by centering on habit-producing practices around the human body, my approach contributes to the analysis of the politics of life in two ways: 1) to understand how human practices around the body change the nature of relations of different scales of reality by triggering new processes and 2) by explaining how objects set conditions for the production of new regimes of perception and politically charged subjectivity. This means the practice reorganizes relations within, between, and about human bodies and redirects our own conscious understandings and decisions about life.

Molecular process

By the first half of twentieth century, scientific, industrial, and popular discourses had a particular encounter that would change the way we eat. As Coole and Frost explain, "Before mapping the genome, many had imagined that each gene produces a corresponding protein that is responsible for a specific trait: a distinctly mechanistic conception of the work of genes" (2010, 17). Landecker explains that from these early assumptions, we inherit the linearity of central dogma – DNA makes RNA, which makes protein. In more recent times, such dogma "is being corrected by the elaboration of other complex temporal and spatial relationships between biological molecules that are ordered by the structure and function of the living cell" (2007, 4), which we know as the field of epigenetics. However, in public and industrial spheres, the centrality of protein was immediately and permanently adopted.

It was Justus von Liebig, who claimed that "muscular energy is the direct product of the ingestion and metabolism of protein", and this claim was followed by "Max Rubner's conclusive correction that animal heat derives not from a substance but from a measurable unit of energy called a calorie" (Lavin, 2013, 51). DNA's assumed linear relation with protein, joined the also inherited discourses of thermodynamics that supported the argument that the body needs of a source of energy to be combusted and then to realize work. Energy processing was understood as the principal for industrial progress and then as a principal for the subject/body (see Rabinbach, 1992). The logic was rather simple: Animals (including humans) need protein to live, and human beings need to eat animals to get that protein, so by the first half of twentieth century, protein became the source and currency of life. Industry took this discourse to promote the consumption of meat, poultry, and animal products in general, arguing that animal protein was the highest-quality protein and then necessary to good health. As any industry enterprise in twentieth-century capitalism, the meat industry strongly tried to reduce the costs and increase the production, and that resulted in the methods that we know today and against to which veganism protest.

But, here is the interesting part: Even when vegans decided to not participate in the industry of meat production due to the cruelty toward animals, they, still to this day, follow the industrial/scientific discourse of the middle twentieth century, which means they still consider protein the cornerstone of nutrition and good health. Yet as we have learned from molecular biology, protein is just one of the three macronutrients that the human body obtains for food, along with carbohydrates and fat. These are "macro" in the sense that they comprise almost all of the weight and calories of food. Vitamins and minerals are the micronutrients. But as we have mentioned, protein was understood to be the most important for health and nutrition, so vegans, still under that assumption, eat trying to compensate the "good quality" of animal protein with vegetal protein. Vegan diet is still a "substance-centered" diet rooted in the thermodynamics and early DNA discourses that identified protein as the main source of energy of the body and animal protein as the highest-quality protein that humans can consume.

The main difference between animal and vegetal proteins are their architectures and shapes, given by the amino acid profile, which is the external structure of which protein is made, that is, the building blocks of proteins (Whitfort, 2005). The reason animal protein was understood to be of better quality is because its amino acid profile is more similar to human proteins, and the process of synthesis works in a more efficient way – meaning faster in the logic of industrial production and progress. It does not mean that vegetal protein does not do the work; it is just that it needs more time to do it and takes more proteins to cover the "required" or "ideal" quantity of protein. As Campbell (2013) – one of the favorite medical defenders of veganism – argues, the amino acid profile

> direct[s] the rates at which the absorbed amino acids are put to use within the body. Animal based proteins, of course, are much more similar to our proteins, thus are used more readily and rapidly than plant proteins. That is, "substrate" amino acids derived from animal-based proteins are more readily available for our own protein synthesizing reactions which allows them to operate at full tilt. Plant proteins are somewhat compromised by their limitation of one or more amino acids. When we restore the relatively deficient amino acid in a plant protein, we get a response rate equivalent to animal proteins.

The protein-centered logic of veganism puts at the center of metabolic processes the interaction between the vegetal protein from food and the animal protein from the human body trying to absorb them. The consequence of this is a monopolization of the rhythm of the protein synthesis, a "slowing down" of the rhythm of protein synthesis due to the presence of exclusively vegetal protein. Even if the quantities and amino acid qualities of the vegan diet are "restored", as Campbell suggests, to guarantee the protein requirements, the rhythm of protein synthesis is subjected to the amino acid profile of vegetal protein, and given that the proteins in our bodies are always animal proteins, such a rhythm is irremediably going to slow down.

In last few years, science has simultaneously proven and disproven the benefits and damages of a diet centered on vegetal protein,[3] as it has also proven and disproven the benefits and damages of animal protein.[4] The conclusion seems clear: We don't know. And even more, nutrition and health seem to be not driven by the virtues or flows of one substance or even the much-heralded protein and its relevance to eating. Then it seems that the preference for one or another kind of protein is rooted in emotional and ideological commitments that find a shortcut for legitimation in scientific models of linear causality encouraging a "substance-centered" acceptance or rejection of veganism. But both cases seem to neglect the ecology of the organism and overemphasize the role and agency of proteins.

What is important to understand about the molecular politics of veganism is the fact that vegetal proteins, with their different amino acid profiles, have the capacity to modify the rhythm of protein synthesis. They bring about information that affects the dynamics of human bodies. That is what Clough (2008) means by the bio-mediated body, a body radically open to outside information. In this sense, food shouldn't be understood as energy coming into the body whose main function is keep the body working, as early models suggested. Rather, as Landecker proposes, food is information capable of modifying metabolism all the way down to DNA, and metabolism is understood as a regulatory interface shaped by the environment. For epigenetics, "these scientific shifts in the understanding of metabolism simultaneously constitute a molecular politics of eating" (Landecker, 2011, 167–168). If previous ideas of metabolism call for a relationality of survival, where food allows bodies to stay alive and most importantly to get energy to work, epigenetics points to a deep transformation: an ontological one. Assuming the idea of food as a signal of epigenetics and the status of food as environmental, different diets might get us to an ontological shift even deeper than changes in molecular patterns.

The molecular politics of veganism are not about an external structure of power. It is not somebody else; it is not even your (vegan)self who is deciding what the rhythm of the pattern in proteins synthesis is going to be. As Frost argues, proteins have "direction without intention" (2016, 90). For the conscious vegan self who decides to intake exclusively vegetal protein, the effects of those proteins in the body simply escape conscious deliberation.

Haptic objects

As explained in the introduction, the aesthetic dimension connecting molecular and organic scales is made of haptic objects. For Harman, all objects are clusters of objects containing real qualities that withdraw from the encounter and sensual qualities that participate in the interaction with other objects. In the introduction of the book, I have described haptic objects as human-emanated objects whose sensual qualities are intensified. Haptic objects are objects belonging to or emanating from the body, such as odor, texture of the skin, the color of the eyes or hair, etc. These are objects participating of relations through sensual qualities and therefore trigger a first level of subjectivity on the other object of the relation, the object that perceives. Haptic objects emerge out of relations among other objects, where a regime of activity has been established – like the politics of slowing down in molecular scale – having as a consequence the intensification of the sensual qualities in the emerging haptic object. These objects emerge as qualities of the body that are not consciously managed but consciously registered – perceptible – like the smell of the body or the texture of the skin. Vegan bodies reorient the potential and the qualities of their bodies in organoleptic domains whose promiscuity make them almost automatically public, prone to be part of encounters with other bodies. These reorientations permeate the politics of their encounters; vegan bodies are bodies of resonance of different qualities, and they might work as disruptive organisms. Haptic objects trigger pure affective experience, not yet the representation of conscious socialization of those qualities.

Harman's OOO (2005) posits that "aesthetics is first philosophy", and further, "causality is alluring". In that vein, Morton (2012) pointed out that causality belongs to aesthetic dimension. Outside OOO, it has also been suggested that aesthetic is political as it reorients the regime of perception, that is, to make perceptible something that was previously not (Rancière, 2014). Inspired by this idea, Panagia has argued that political life is fundamentally a perceptual enterprise. Panagia's most provocative proposition is "that the first political act is also an aesthetic one, a partitioning of sensation that divides the body and its organs of sense perception and assigns to them corresponding capacities for the making of sense" (2009, 9). However, the condition of possibility for this reorientation of perception is the existence of an object with intensified sensual qualities capable of causing variations in perceptual domain by triggering other sensations the body is used to. Sensation gives us entrance to the world of encounters precisely by the interruption of prestructured sense, or what Rancière calls "dissensus". Senses are political because they reconfigure the organization of the body; the organoleptic properties redirect their attention toward something that was not holding the privilege of being filtered by perception. Massumi has also pointed out the dissensual character of aesthetics and its political potential, where affective politics "holds contrasting alternatives together without immediately demanding that one alternative eventuate and the others evaporate" (2015b, 68).

It is not "out of scale" to speculate about vegan molecular politics as the condition of possibility for modifications and the emergence of sensual qualities of haptic objects emanating from vegan bodies, particularly smell and the texture of the skin of vegan organisms. Those two haptic components are reoriented in vegan bodies and represent political action through sensation. Smell and texture are deeply intertwined. They are vectors between molecular and organic scales, but they are also vectors between the inside and the outside of the body; alteration on their aesthetic properties have incidence in the perceptual domain of other bodies, especially non-vegan bodies.

In science, body odor is commonly attributed to genetic factors. There is, however, agreement on certain environmental factors that modify body odor, where diet is the most significant source of environmental variability (Roberts et al., 2005; Havlicek and Lenochova, 2008). In cultural theory there is also large agreement on the relation between diet and body smell, and it has been addressed regarding its effects in terms of class, gender, and race in Western societies and its difference with non-Western societies (Classen et al., 1994). Havlicek and Lenochova (2008) have conducted more specific research to compare the smells of bodies under meat and meat-free diets, finding that the "odor of donors when on the non-meat diet was rated more pleasant, attractive and less intense" (Havlicek and Lenochova, 2008, 204). Potts and Parry (2010) have also explored what they call "Vegansexuality", where the difference in smell between vegans and meat eaters is considered a concern of attractiveness. In addition to this, there are endless conversations in online forums in which vegans and non-vegans have discussed the difference on smell emanation and smell perception. Take, for example, the discussion on vegan smell in the veganforum.com from June 12, 2008. Comments such as this can be found on this forum: "[W]hen I turned vegan 3 years ago after about a week I noticed that I could see better, smell better and my wee tasted better". Diet affects smell, and that is more notorious when there is a consistent aspect of diet. It does not mean that all vegans eat the same, for there are endless possibilities of food that exclude animal products. Yet that is precisely the constant, the lack of meat, which renders a particular odor signature.

Teresa Brennan (2004) explains that smell is the key to understanding the way in which the social shapes the biological. For her, pheromones carry information from one body to another as a way of socialization. Jablonski (2006) has described the effects of different diets in the skin as cultures in which the diet is high in vegetables and people are prone to show healthier skin. Fruits and vegetables are rich in fiber, antioxidants, phytonutrients, and minerals, and they contain more water than any other food, all of which are strongly associated with healthy skin. But vegans do not all eat the same, for the skin modifications are related to nonanimal eating and might vary as a function of what food is substituting the animal food. In online blogs and forums, vegans have expressed their skin changes. Take, for example, the xovain.com blog entry from June 20, 2014: "My skin feels 'glowier' and more radiant than ever before. It's like I've suddenly received through broccoli and strawberries what I was never able to get through a thousand overpriced and underwhelming serums, masks, lotions, and creams". There is also a strong association in online discourses between veganism and beauty, as in thesexyveggie.com blog. From an October 13, 2014, entry: "Maybe this is the best thing I could be doing for my skin and my overall aging process after all! I mean, a plant-based diet is chock full of all of the nutrients needed for fresh, healthy skin. I am feeding my skin everything it needs to be healthy and glowing – from the inside out." In dating websites for vegans like vgirlsvguys or veganpassions, it is common to read that they are looking for a "vegan skin". According to those websites, vegan skin looks different – mainly compared with a non-vegan version. It looks less porous, its brightness softens, and its color intensifies. Smell and texture in vegan bodies are haptic objects relating through sensual qualities and, then, reformulating encounters. Haptic objects of vegan bodies might require special attention. It is not an imposition to the perceptual domain; rather, it is a gift for those who want to note it: the gift of experiencing a different body.

Following Panagia, senses presuppose a specific organization of the body that organolepsis can break through new experiences. But such a dissensus is rooted in material life; what is at stake in the political life of vegan touch and smell is the possibility of the properties and qualities of the food becoming properties and qualities of the vegan body. The eating practice generates intimacy with matter, which then makes it possible to trigger the patterns of activity contained in such matter to be taken up in your body. Touching these reoriented vegan properties makes us face the boundaries of the sovereign organism; touching creates individuality and at the same time dissolves it. Then the reorientation of touch by the modification of the texture of the skin calls attention to a neglected element that is precisely about the boundary of the political subject. If our food is capable of changing or intensifying some of the sensual qualities of the haptic objects of our bodies, and such changes can be read as a reorientation of potential crucial for political life and for perceptual regimes, then the boundaries of the sovereign subject once represented by the organism are no longer that clear. Lavin (2013) uses the term "ontopolitical fiction" to refer to this impossibility to understand political life as a matter of a self-contained, secure-bordered, conscious, deliberating organism. Haptic objects as a political dimension of veganism make manifest the relations between food materiality and the human body as a condition of possibility of events of dissensus.

The advantage of reading smell and skin as haptic objects is to see the political effects of a concrete object that, even if they emerge out of processual activity at certain scales of reality, they are no longer part of the permanent becoming of the process. It has already become a stable object – a steady point of reality that deserves to be analyzed as such.

Organic process

The organic scale of reality is the domain of conscious deliberation. Organic politics refer to consciously driven practices of everyday life and constructions of self-identity. The vegan organism goes through a process of becoming vegan in which it needs to pursue and actively construct the vegan world through new ways of doing and thinking about the self. As Wright (2015) argues, veganism is at once both identity and practice. To refer to the politics of formation of such identity and practice in the organic scale, I use the term "politics of tracking".

The fact that amino acid profiles in vegetal and animal proteins are not the same results in a need of compensation of proteins or at least more careful attention to the quantity and the quality of vegetal proteins that vegan bodies are consuming. Then, the policy of slowing down in the molecular scale is at the same time a condition of possibility and a consequence of the politics of tracking in the organic scale. The vegan organism, along with their renovated haptic objects, consciously tracks the vegetal protein to maintain an organic commitment with the politics of veganism. Vegans usually are aware of the places they can go to have lunch or dinner, and the supermarkets that supply vegan products, or even the vegan alternatives within non-vegan spaces like regular restaurants or supermarkets. But vegans will also track social relations, people to share ideas with, a couple of vegan friends, a blog online; it is, in short, a vegan community. The tracking of the vegan lifestyle is mandatory, so to know their options they construct a sort of vegan cartography of the city involving substances, people, places, and so on. The organic politics of tracking also involves the tracking of vegan personal boundaries, what I will call the "vegan self". Not all vegans practice veganism in the same way (Greenebaum, 2012); for some veganism goes way beyond eating and includes concerns about clothing, cleaning products, makeup, and so on. For others food exceptions are allowed. Some vegans would allow themselves to eat honey, whereas for others that may be unthinkable. Someone might make exceptions when traveling because of not having done a vegan mapping of the city. All those represent just some of the things the vegan has to think about. These are the politics of interaction with substances, places, and people that delineate the boundaries vegan identity/practice while perpetuating the molecular politics of slowing down.

Wright suggests that to think about the vegan identity, we should consider the fact that not all vegans become vegans for the same reason. The ethical concern about exploitation of animals is the most popular reason, but there are also vegans who have changed for health, religious, or environmental reasons, among others. Veganism thus is at once practice and identity at the core of political life. As Lavin explains, "[E]ating thus not only helps constitute the self but also constitutes one's sense of self" (2013, xxx). Massumi refers to this practice/identity as a form of habit with affective potential; he suggests that "[i]t's a way of acquiring new propensities. . . .[W]e become aware that they function, even if we are not aware of them as they function". Massumi further posits that this practice as habit is "taking 'me' to be the relational matrix of reactivation that my body carries forward", so the repetition of this practice is what shapes identity. In his words, "I do not contract habits. Habits contract to form me" (2015b, 64–65).

The vegan self works at the organic-conscious scale of activity in which conscious politics and alleged free deliberation are played in making decisions about the boundaries of vegan practice and identity. The vegan self is constantly constructed through such practices; rendering vegan a processual self embedded in a system of tracking practices and identity from relations with matter. Thus matter is at the center of the logic of tracking, and subjectivity is embedded in our material relations.

Organic politics of tracking are "substance-centered" politics. Whereas vegans also track places, community, and even a version of themselves, the criteria for tracking is a substance: vegan food. But because organic politics are driven by conscious activity, the fact that conscious politics depend on relations with matter speaks out of our fake boundaries as liberal subjects. Food politics attempts to safeguard the illusion of a safe boundary, a political subject separated from the world charged with plenty of freedom and self-determination through conscious deliberation. Lavin proposes to understand the politics of food not as a strictly cultural politic but to see how it is rooted in personal anxiety that results from political concerns – an effort to "track" the pieces of freedom in a context in which, as he says, the only field of life still offering freedom is the market. For Lavin, the politics of food is the result of personal anxieties originated by political structural conditions. It is the necessity of shaping an identity that attempts to respond to such structure; so the ideas promoting responsible consumerism on self-reliance and self-governance resonate with the neoliberal trend toward market supremacy and individual responsibility.

That is the peril of organic politics – the focus on control and power and its immediate connection with conscious deliberation. The organic politics of veganism are the liberal politics of the free market embedded in a discourse of compassion that sediments even more the sense of individuality of the liberal democratic subject. Vegan politics of tracking are under the illusion of the liberal sovereign subject belonging to the free market while shaping – through practice and identity – the organic scale of our cross-scalar account of politics of life.

Aesthetic objects

Connecting the organic and cultural scales, we have the aesthetic objects. These are objects involved in vegan practices at the organic scale, such as vegan restaurants, vegan products, and vegan dishes. Aesthetic objects are consciously produced and socialized vegan objects, so they relate through their sensual qualities; however, their real qualities remain behind human conscious experience. Based on Harman's quadruple object, aesthetic objects are sensual objects whose sensual qualities connect to allure; they create a backdrop for sensual encounters that call the subject to the domain of imperceptible reality. What is interesting then about aesthetic objects is not their relation with human perceptual apparatus but the relations among them, object–object, and the subsequent objects emerging from those relations, which I equate with what affect studies has called "atmospheres" (Anderson, 2009; Stewart, 2011). An atmosphere here is an object resulting out of the interaction of the sensual qualities of aesthetic objects. An atmosphere is what Harman calls a real object with sensual qualities. As such, it is withdrawn from the encounter; however, human bodies are compelled to feel something that has otherwise escaped from the perceptual regime. The sensual qualities of aesthetic objects participate on assembling a particular aesthetic to vegan culture, the vegan atmosphere, that redirects the regime of perception of the vegan community. This is a highly affective dimension of political life that works as the common ground for the sensibility that will constitute the common sense of vegan ideology. The atmosphere emerging out of the relations of aesthetic objects provides sensual qualities to vegan ideology; this is the way such ideology looks, the way it feels, its textures, in short the material backdrop of veganism shaped by aesthetic objects.

We can cite as a first example the design of vegan dishes. The way vegan food looks is half substance and half design; for example, vegan desserts lack the fluffiness of omnivorous desserts because they are not made with milk, butter, and eggs, making dessert textures more porous. Something similar happens with quiches and other baked vegan dishes; baking vegan ingredients results in sort of rustic appearance. This, along with the green and sometimes raw vegetal colors in such plates, results in a nature-evoking appearance. At least in New York City this joins the trend of investing in visual designs for plating food that have been common in gastronomy since the 1990s: tall ornaments at the top, sauce mirrors at the bottom, sprinkle colors in the middle. Vegan dishes hold an aesthetic that evokes nature at the same time that looks cool (see Figure 2.1).

These sensual qualities are followed by the similar motifs in vegan restaurants in which the nature-evoking quality is followed by two particularities that help constitute a vegan atmosphere: There are always books and spiritual motifs from vegan recipes to vegan manifestos, manuals, and all kinds of vegan literature, to different kind of spiritual allegory, like Buddhist, Rastafarian, mandala-like images or symbols of peace standing in phrases, posters, logos, and so on (see Figure 2.2). Such a disposition of material elements stands as the material backdrop of some ideas: Vegans read, love nature, and are spiritual people. Another set of aesthetic objects are vegan products. In addition to joining the nature-evoking motif though the colors and images they use in their labels (see Figure 2.3), vegan products add to the atmosphere statements in the design that contribute to shaping the material base of vegan sensibility. Vegan products state things like "cruelty free", "not tested in animals",

Figure 2.1 Vegan dishes looking vegan

"no animal ingredients", and even the more common "100% natural" or "organic". The naming is at the same time an aesthetic and ideological element; it is also present in the names of places and dishes. Restaurant and motifs described here come from vegan restaurants in New York City, such as Peacefood Café with dishes like Beyond Chicken Basket or the Protein-Packed Kale Salad, making spiritual/ideological, animal-free, and healthy claims. There is also the Candle Café, whose logo shows a leaf emanating light rays, offering dishes like the Green Goodess or a section in the menu called Pharmacy offering Juice to Heal, to cite a couple of representative examples. In this respect, Timothy Morton suggests that "green consumerism made it possible to be both pro-capitalist and green" (2009, 110).

Figure 2.2 Books, spiritual allegories, and plants in vegan restaurants

Figure 2.3 Nature-evoking aesthetics in vegan products

All those qualities of vegan objects contribute to shaping the vegan atmosphere. The aesthetic objects and the atmosphere they create constitute what Panagia (2009) calls a "particular dynamic of the sensible" that determines the conditions through and which we might sense the world and those who occupy it. As he suggests, the micropolitical strategy of such regimes of perception creates "dynamics of conviction that generate affinities of sensibility between and among individuals and groups" (24). These regimes of perception constitute a common world of the sensible that "at one and the same time, distributes legitimacy and endorses the convictions that bring that sense world into being" (24). Kathleen Stewart (2011) has coined the term "atmospheric attunement" to explain this sort of affective force with material basis that affects our understanding of the world. Atmospheric attunements represent sensitive responses to emergent forms. If the aesthetic properties of these objects modify the regime of perception, then we can see how the aesthetic reorientation works as a backdrop for subjectivity and signification.

The most important consequence of aesthetic objects is not the representation that comes from them; it is rather the fact that they establish a shared sensation, and vegan bodies get oriented to a new sensorial regime, getting to feel veganism even without the food. Simply through the aesthetics of the objects involved in the practice, vegans get to feel vegan.

Cultural process

Cultural politics refers to the regime of relations established by official institutions representing vegan ideology, such as the Vegan Society[5] and the American Vegan Society[6] (AVS). They work to build an official version of the practice and the identity of being vegan. To refer the political regime set by these institutions, I use the following term: "Politics of Compassion".

Moran explores the different changes in defining veganism by the Vegan Society. What is notable in her analysis is that veganism is defined at the beginning as an eating practice and starts changing slowly through the years, until it turns into a politics of "compassion and reverence for life and avoidance of exploitation" (1985, 18–19), in which the eating aspect happens to be almost secondary. As stated in its website, the AVS is "a nonprofit, nonsectarian, nonpolitical, tax-exempt educational membership organization teaching a compassionate way of living by reverence for life and ahimsa".[7] We get to see how the official and institutionalized version of veganism goes way beyond an eating practice, for it is rather a moral project revolving around this version of compassion. The vegan subject is also defined by this version of compassion: "Vegan is eating only from the plant kingdom; making conscious, compassionate choices about food". Thus a change is introduced in the cultural scale.

Rather than the vegan being simultaneously a practice and an identity like Wright (2015) suggests, in the institutional version the vegan is an identity gained through and subjected to a practice with an emotional implication. For AVS you are not vegan until you compassionately stop eating animals.

Compassion has gained attention in political theory in the last few years with particular attention to compassion as one of the most salient emotions in political life (see Ure and Frost, 2014; Thompson and Hoggett, 2012). Berlant defines compassion as an "emotion in operation" that is necessarily denoting privilege: "[T]he suffer is over there" (2004, 4). It follows that compassion involves the awareness of the value of compassion as well as the value of the compassionate one. Compassion then involves a sense of obligation to respond to somebody else's conditions. As an emotion, compassion is irremediably linked to the identity of the holder and to the construction of that identity because it necessarily involves a cognitive and reflexive process. Nassbaum (2001) believes that compassion can have a cognitive edge; she sees compassion as an emotional bridge between the individual and the community – "a bridge to justice". Coetzee (1999) does not exclude nonhumans from such a sense of justice, for he has argued that this sense of obligation of action and the feeling of somebody else's pain can even extend to animals: We can sympathetically imagine their pain and feel compassion for them.

In veganism, decisions about diet are the basis of the practice through which vegans gain their identity because, in all these descriptions of ahimsa and reverence for life, the only thing that is described clearly is what you can and cannot eat. Eating a plant-based diet is represented as a compassionate way to live; and then, in opposition, eating meat or animal products is understood as participating in the harming and cruel methods of industry. Thus, compassion becomes a practice, "an emotion in operation", whose specificity is constrained to the abstinence of meat and animal products. In such a compassionate practice, "reverence for life" involves a "don't kill, don't eat animals", a "don't touch policy". Even more, the "dynamic harmlessness" of vegan compassion is about "avoiding" the relation of the vegan subject with the harming practice, so they can gain their vegan identity, but it doesn't address the structural problem of the cause of such animal suffering. Any latent assumption that not harming has a wider impact is based on the illusion that the sum of individual wills will eventually change the social structure.

If political agency is socially distributed, as Krause suggests, in terms of human agency such a distributed quality means that the impact of the actions of a subject depend on how they are picked up by others.

It follows that the awarding of responsibility given to the politics of compassion – because of its capacity to respond to someone else's pain – is still very much under the idea of responsibility and agency of the sovereign individual. For Krause, the distinction between identity and will is crucial. The former should not be reduced to the latter; otherwise, human agency is not properly understood as distributed. The problem then with the vegan version of compassion as stated by vegan institutions is that it ties up a specific practice with an identity revolving around an emotion. In this logic, being a compassionate person can be demonstrated through your eating policies, and the reason behind your eating policies cannot be other than compassion, amhisa, and reverence for life. As we saw at the organic scale, vegans do whatever they want and for the reasons that better suit them; compassion alone does not explain veganism. However, the vegan cultural politics of compassion still hold a restrictive character. Compassion is not understood in the broader sense as a political virtue or as feeling the pain of somebody else and then the desire to help. The vegan politics of compassion states that the way of helping, the only way to be compassionate, is by taking distance from those in pain. "Do not eat animals" is not necessarily improving the conditions we create for them; it is rather just not eating them. To be even clearer, taking another kind of action to improve animals' conditions while still eating animals does not qualify as compassion for AVS precisely because for AVS veganism is not about animal well-being; it is about sharing moral standards. If the sense of responsibility is limited by a specific practice, agency is completely located in the will of the subject that might or might not accomplish such a practice. By limiting the evidence of compassion to your diet decisions, vegan institutions strengthen the idea of a free will subject, and at the same time they restrict the way to be the right liberal subject, setting emotional conditions on the way responsibility is to be taken. In the cultural scale, compassion as a specific emotion attempts to regulate the relation between practice and identity that the subject executes freely in the organic scale.

Compassion conveys its quota of self-complacency through looking for the well-being of others; in the case of veganism, it points to an almost martyrization of both the compassionate vegan and the neglected animal. But as the policy is about "avoiding", it could be said that because the animal is still dead, what is being avoided is the guilt and pain of being part of the killing/eating. Thus, vegan compassion is at the end of the day a sort of self-compassion trying to ameliorate as well the potential self-human suffering or potential guilt. Yet behind the vegan politics of compassion, there is a sense of resistance to injustice that supposes to be the function of compassion as political virtue, although resistance has its own problems. Massumi has addressed the restrictive character of some ideas about resistance as political movements. In his understanding, an "ought" to resist is already a position of servitude to a higher order. For Massumi the sense of obligation "carries seeds of domination – perhaps a new order of domination", he says, "but domination nonetheless". "Freedom, like oppression, is desired, or it is nothing at all. It cannot be 'oughted' and imposed. It cannot be inculcated. It is desired, or it is nothing" (2015b, 106–107).

Compassion has potential in theory and practice to improve political life, but this potential lies mainly in its claim of dissolving the boundary between the compassionate one and the one in pain and thus expanding the notion of political responsibility outside the domain of conscious deliberation. Although improving the conditions of the lives of animals and avoiding slaughtering sound necessary, establishing a regime of compassion seems to encourage a compulsive and easily naïve regime in which the human subject is understood as the currency of political agency. Subjects changing their diet will not solve structural causes of animal suffering; the cultural scale of veganism pretends to deal with structural forces operating in the cultural scale by alienating the wills in the organic scale. Structuring vegan ideology around the idea of compassion and reverence for life sets out straightforward assumptions that do not help develop a much-needed critical compassion.

Politics beyond consciousness

I have proposed a way to understand the political dimension of eating in terms of a complex cross-scalar system involving processes and objects. On the one hand, addressing the dynamism of relations helps us embrace the process-centered[8] contributions of bodies of thought such as affect studies and new materialism. On the other hand, the idea of objects as events that reorient human perception and sensibility helps us think about the qualities of objects and their political implications, a perspective closer to the concerns of object-oriented thinking. A cross-scalar account of the politics of eating using the example of veganism makes clear what Bennett (2010) might call assemblages made of human and nonhuman components. As this chapter has shown, the politics of veganism are made of diverse components, including substances, practices, places, smells, textures, colors, communities, exceptions, ideologies, emotions, amino acid profiles, molecular rhythms, designs of dishes and places, human body/mind vegan interactions, identities, practices, and institutions, all of them interacting in a complex way and embedded in different, coexisting regimes of regulation and having different effects on one another. It is noteworthy that recognizing different scales of reality and different kinds of objects participating in political life has required taking seriously what Clough (2008) refers to as the informative capacity of matter. Thinking about the relational and aesthetic properties of matter in (at least) three scales of reality and two aesthetic dimensions is necessary to achieve a sense of the complexity of the political life of veganism if we are to move out of the notions of agency, responsibility, free will, and liberal subjects hitherto explored in traditional approaches.

Politics does not involve exclusively the self-exercising sovereign agency and its direct effects in the world. Political life cannot be reduced to a "conscious" exercise of the production of a political identity; neither does it deserve to be concerned exclusively with the study of relations of power, dominance, or exclusion, whether they include institutions or not. As veganism helps demonstrate, political life in an everyday practice might also involve ontological molecular becomings, haptic and aesthetic reorientations, everyday tracking, and cultural politics. It is for that reason that this expansion is needed. Understanding the politics of life beyond sovereignty and identity politics represents the challenge of approaching human life by simultaneously stepping away from it. A cross-scalar politics of life might at the very least set some steady coordinates that help track differentiated dynamics and regimes of activity operating at different scales of reality. At the same time, the inclusion of objects allows us to look at the reorientation of perception and sensibility as politically charged events. If eating serves as a practice to illustrate this model, my hope is that could be taken to analyze any practice whose epicenter is the human body.

Notes

1 New materialism includes a broad spectrum of perspectives emerging form fields such as political theory, feminist studies, and science and technology studies. Among the main exponents are Elizabeth Grosz's biological-inspired vibrational ontologies, *The Nick of Time. Politics Evolution and the Untimely* (Durham: Duke University Press, 2004); Karen Barad's Agencial Realism, *Meeting the Universe Half Way. Quantum Physics and the Entanglement of Matter and Meaning* (Durham: Duke University Press, 2007); Janne Bannett and her Vital Materialism: *Vibrant Matter. A Political Ecology of Things* (Durham: Duke University Press, 2010); and Rossi Braidotti's posthuman approach, *The Posthuman* (Malden: Polity, 2013). For an overview of main authors and especially the intersection between new materialism and feminist studies, see Stacy Alaimo and Susan Hekman, *Material Feminisms* (Bloomington: Indiana University Press, 2008); for a review of the history and current state of new materialism, featuring especially Manuel DeLanda and

Quentin Meillassoux, see Rick Dolphijn and Iris van der Tuin, *New Materialism: Interviews & Cartographies* (Michigan: Open Humanities Press, 2012).

2 One of the reasons aesthetic dimensions are so important in accounting for political life is for their relation with the political economy; as Steven Shaviro explains it, "[A]esthetics exist in a special relationship to political economy, precisely because aesthetics is the one thing that cannot be reduced to political economy. Politics, ethics, epistemology, and even ontology are all subject to 'determination in the last instance' by the forces and relations of production. On a human scale, this is Marx's central thesis; but it also holds true on a cosmic scale, where the determining forces and relations are those described by subatomic physics and thermodynamics. Aesthetics is the lone exception to this rule; it does not violate the "laws" of political and physical economy, but it oddly subsists alongside these economies and apart from them." Steven Shaviro, *No Speed Limit. Three Essays on Accelerationism* (Minneapolis: University of Minnesota Press, 2015), 25. If aesthetics is not cognitive, not conscious/organic, not in its policies, not for its regulation, at least aesthetic properties of human bodies under a regime of vegan molecular politics cannot be consciously controlled, then these aesthetic qualities escape from the liberal ontopolitics proposed by Levin. These qualities illustrate what he call the fiction of liberal ontopolitics that presuppose a well-contained and regulated subject.

3 On the benefits of a vegetal protein-based diet, see: Philip J. Tuso et al., 2013. On the other hand, for the perils of vegetal protein diets, particularly the much-heralded critique on the lack of B12 vitamins, see, Roman Pawlak et al., 2013.

4 On the perils of animal protein, you can see Lagiou et al., 2012. On the other hand, for the benefits of animal proteins, see Paddon-Jones, 2015.

5 www.vegansociety.com/

6 www.americanvegan.org/

7 According to the AVS website "Ahimsa is a Sanskrit word for non-killing and non-harming. It is not mere passivity, but a positive method of meeting the dilemmas and decisions of daily life. In the western world, we call it dynamic harmlessness, which encourages nonviolent action to create positive changes. The six pillars of this dynamic philosophy for modern life (one for each letter of A-H-I-M-S-A) are: Abstinence from animal products; Harmlessness with reverence for life; Integrity of thought, word, and deed; Mastery over oneself; Service to humanity, nature, and creation; Advancement of understanding and truth".

8 For a review on process philosophies as the philosophical base of affect studies, particularly for the case of Deleuze, Bergson, and Whitehead, see Lara 2015.

3 Chocolate and desire

Now that almost all our units have been introduced: the three scales in Chapters 1 and 2 and our three objects in Chapter 2. In this chapter I want to concentrate on the way in which the object-mediated relation of our three scales of reality affects subjectivity. To do this I'm going to expose the production of desire around chocolate as it happened to me when living in Brooklyn.

Before entering the relationship among our three scales, let me clarify something about the study of subjectivity as it is in current critical theory. In the last twenty years, affect studies has prompted scholarly attention to turn to the nonconscious processes at play in experience. By exploring domains other than consciousness, we have been lured to delve into the processes that occur at small scales in both organic and material/nonhuman becomings alike, mediating and participating in complex entanglements with embodied human experience (Gregg and Seigworth, 2010; Clough, 2012). In that vein, affect studies has reencountered scientific expressions and some of the so-called process philosophies (Blackman and Venn, 2010; Lara, 2015). Particularly, encounters with the neurosciences, mainly the works of Damasio and LeDoux, have brought enthusiasts and critics alike (Damasio, 2003; LeDoux, 1998).[1] However, affect studies' insights on nondiscursive, nonrepresentational, nonconscious activity still need to be understood in relation to other conscious and cultural processes, or at least, such a relation requires further exploration to comprehend complex processes emerging out of the concatenation of events at different scales of the reality. In what follows I take the case of food craving, understood as a sudden desire for specific food, to explore how desire production emerges from an assemblage made from multiple agents and events, where conscious activity is but one among other, sometimes stronger capacities. I give special attention to the restrictive capacities of consciousness commonly executed in the event of the craving, and I ask: Other than exercising a restrictive capacity, what influence does consciousness have on cravings?

In nutritional science, Annemarie Mol's study of food cravings contrasts two different approaches that are concerned with weight loss and obesity. On the one hand are dieting techniques of control in which the main idea is that you should "mind your plate", and on the other are dieting techniques of care in which the main idea is that to "enjoy your food" (Mol, 2012, 2013a, 2013b; Vogel and Mol, 2014). As Mol suggests, "mind your plate" approaches always involve the idea that "a person who wants to lose weight needs to overrule the desires of her craving body. Her mind has to put itself in a sovereign position and make 'good choices' about what to eat" (Mol, 2012, 379). Such a model encourages a sort of "homeostatic eating" that allows the body to stay the same (see also Turner, 1996; Jallinoja et al., 2010). In opposition, "enjoy your food" approaches believe that from propitiating pleasure emerges the possibility of "a body that when it 'feels that it has eaten' stops eating without having been told to do so. It no longer craves for more, as it is satisfied" (Mol, 2012, 388). This model encourages what she calls a "hedonistic eating" where the priority is creating pleasure (see, e.g., Rozin, 1999; Willson, 2005). Mol recognizes also that social sciences have adopted this tension between health and pleasure and have taken it for granted: "While these views are in opposition to one another, a similar scheme is at work in both: rationality and control are disentangled from, and contrasted with, desire and excess" (Vogel and Mol, 2014, 306). Such a strongly defined division leaves no space to think about the production of pleasure as a powerful resource in managing desire production by means other than the repression of such a desire.

For Krause (2015), the idea of personal sovereignty involves at the same time the rational capacity for self-control and a normative claim about the right of such control. In a similar vein, Lavin (2013) uses the term "ontopolitical fiction" to refer to the illusion of a boundary defined by the organism and regulated through conscious deliberation. Such an ontopolitical fiction allows us to ignore relational processes beyond organic and conscious organization. In light of processes that bypass human consciousness, such as cravings, we need to question human consciousness as the epicenter of sovereignty. We should look into the relations at stake in the production of desire to see how we might better construe the function of conscious deliberation. Panagia (2009) has pointed out the political potential of the mouth, not for its capacity to talk but for its capacity to reconfigure the organolepsis of the body, which is to say the qualities of the encounters between subject and food. Thus, behind my interests in looking for other conscious possibilities within the craving assemblage lies the political project of challenging the sovereign status of human consciousness and particularly its status as control device.

I evoke Deleuze and Guattari's assemblage theory to explain the configuration of the chocolate craving, and in the final part of this chapter, I will bring Malabou's ideas of brain plasticity as a conscious resource to diversify the experience of desire. Consciousness, I argue, can act as a disobedience device: a device more capable of using pleasure to diversify the production of desire rather than avoiding pleasure to resist desire. It then becomes clear that pleasure and control are not be in opposition after all. Elsewhere (Lara, 2017), I have argued the speculative potential of experimental writing and how it is particularly good for building theoretical arguments in affect studies. As such, I also include fragments of field notes from one of my own experiences of chocolate craving to illustrate my theoretical argument.

Chocolate-craving assemblage

I am taking a walk through my neighborhood in Brooklyn. With my mind on my own affairs, I fail to notice a chocolate store along my path. Yet, as I pass, the aroma of fresh chocolate billows into the street and wafts in my direction, or so my nose is telling me. I feel the smell of chocolate. No longer my affairs, it is chocolate on my mind, a familiar scent, to be sure, but no less intoxicating. I turn my head, and for the first time, the chocolate store is in my sight. I enter, and just as quickly I'm eating free samples and looking at their products. After taking a look, I finally get a bar of tangy, dark chocolate and some spicy chocolate powder to prepare drinkable chocolate, as I foresee a cold night. This was not on my day's agenda, but with a sudden desire, my plans have diverged. I have eaten chocolate and gotten more to eat and drink afterward. As I leave the store, I get rid of the chocolate bar wrapper, so I can keep eating as I walk away.

Consider this anecdote. Experiencing such an innocent chocolate craving becomes complicated if, as was the case, I am trying to lose weight. Why didn't I at least deliberate: To eat or not to eat? In light of cravings, how might one make sound decisions when one is suddenly invaded by desire? What forces, other than "willpower", are pushing and pulling on this event? To understand this chocolate craving, it is necessary to recognize that desire is not something that lies in consciousness and so cannot be managed exclusively from there. Instead, desire is an event arising from the productive relations among heterogeneous agents with different natures, functions, and capacities. In the chocolate-craving example, it is possible to recognize at least some of the agencies at stake: the smell, my nose, the store, free samples, my plans, Brooklyn's chocolate topography, and of course the chocolate itself. Each of these must do its part for the event to emerge. Deleuze and Guattari (1977, 1987) coined the term "assemblage" to describe those events in which different agents, human and other-than-human, experience encounters and affect one another. From such encounters emerges a force of production that is the agency of the assemblage, this is to say, what this event can do.

Desire, Deleuze and Guattari (1987) suggest, is the production of assemblages, and it produces assemblages in which consciousness is just one element among many. It follows that the advantage of understanding craving as an assemblage is that doing so allows us to see that it has no center of control. As Bennett has argued, within the assemblage, "no one materiality or type of material has sufficient competence to determine consistently the trajectory or impact of the group" (2010, 24). This means that the agencies entangled in the assemblage participate in the production of desire but are also always exceeded by it.

Although cravings can be triggered by different causes, my craving in the anecdote start with smelling chocolate. Shepherd (2013) has suggested that smell is more important for feeling a taste than taste itself. In his theory of neurogastronomy, flavor is not something that a substance possesses; instead, it is the complex outcome of what he calls the "Human Brain Flavor System". This system is a machinist assemblage connecting molecules of smell, retronasal smell functions, and brain activity to generate a state within a body, which Shepherd recognizes as the sensation of a specific flavor. When we smell, the environment and human body get in touch by the interactions between receptor molecules and molecules of smell. Such interaction is often explained in molecular biology using the metaphor of "lock-and-key",[2] which supposes that smell molecules are like keys that "open" specific receptor molecules. According to this logic, when the key turns the lock, the molecule changes its internal structure. The interaction between smell molecules and receptor molecules, understood in terms of the "lock-and-key" system, has prompted consideration of how the information carried in a sensory stimulus is translated into a representation in the nervous system and, therefore, how it is presented in the brain itself. How does the smell become a craving? Shepherd argues that smell molecules are "represented" in the brain as spatial patterns of activity and that this fact supports the hypothesis of an analogy with the visual system, implying the existence of an "odor image" or "smell image" (2013, 82). It is noteworthy that Shepherd's analogy is a metaphorical one. This means that such a spatial pattern of activity in the brain could be thought of as an image in the sense that is made out of specific networks configured in specific forms, not because the subject produces mental images to represent the smell and then accumulates them as if the story of desire could be stored in images somewhere in the brain. What we have is a personal and neuronal experience adding states to our body's repertory. However, we have to remember that Deleuze was fairly allergic to the idea of the brain as a device of images or representations (Deleuze and Guattari, 1994).

This brain "image" would then also correspond with certain physiological states in the rest of the body. It follows that the anticipation of such physiological states would be a proto-state of the body mediated by the brain. Then, the body's awareness of the forthcoming flavor is due to the brain reading our retronasal smell, so the body can anticipate and desire a potential state. Such an organic invocation can be explained through the so-called mirror neurons, which are generally defined as neurons that fire both when an individual makes a motor action and when they see another actor performing the same action.[3] Victoria Pitts-Taylor (2013) explains that mirror neurons located in brain regions associated with motor action, facial recognition, and somatosensory processing are supposed to allow the brain to simulate certain body states as if they were occurring in the one's own body. Through mirror neurons, Pitts-Taylor suggests, the human capacities for "mind-reading", or understanding another's intentions, and empathy, or feeling what another is feeling, are being rethought as inbuilt, automatic, and prelinguistic neural capacities. For Damasio (2010) the network in which mirror neurons are embedded achieves conceptually what he hypothesized as the "as-if body loop" system, "the simulation, in the brain's body maps, of a body state that is not actually taking place in the organism" (110). But what is even more interesting in Damasio's reading of mirror neuron theory is this suggestion: "If a complex brain can simulate someone else's body states, one assumes that it would be able to simulate its own body states" (2010, 110). A state that has previously occurred in the organism, like an encounter with chocolate, should be more easily simulated because it has already been mapped by precisely the same somato-sensing structures that are now responsible for simulating it. However, because these "as-if body loops" are subtle and fleeting, they are less likely to enter conscious awareness (Cromby, 2007). Damasio suggests that the "as-if system" as applied to others would not have developed had there not been an "as-if system" first applied to the brain's own organism.

Following Damasio's understanding of mirror neurons, we can speculate that my brain has mapped previous encounters between my body and chocolate and that it is easy to evoke the potential sensation of chocolate. In the example of me walking by the chocolate store and feeling the smell, such a smell works as a physiological warning of the potential chocolate experience. This state of evocation, or not-yet-mapped-state, is what Damasio calls a proto-state of the body, understood as a sort of anticipation to whatever the body has felt and mapped before. The proto-state is then an expression of empathy with the past of one's own body. The importance of proposing smell as crucial to the configuration of flavor lies in the fact that molecular components evoking the brain images come before the food gets into the mouth, even before the food falls into our sight, as in the case of my chocolate craving. Proto-states of the body triggered by smell are therefore a part of the assemblage that is clearly not fully controlled by conscious activity. This means that brain activity is modulated and dependent upon the social configuration from which the encounters between bodies occur. As Pitts-Taylor suggests, brain activity is not indifferent to surroundings but rather highly vulnerable to it. The brain is always plastic, always becoming from encounters, so "brain plasticity is a work of culture, an imprint of collective human effort" (Pitts-Taylor, 2016, 40).

Desires for food and its neuro-correlates are necessarily situated within the history of our previous encounters. This is because the maps that the brain creates correspond with certain previous experiences of food and social events that occur within social environments that are also part of our assemblage. Body-brain is processual, plastic, and embedded in a context. We cannot talk about brain functions working homogeneously within those bodies. Nonetheless, some elements of the environment represent a condition of possibility for both molecular transmission and brain mapping and are thus relevant to any account of the chocolate craving assemblage. Berlant (2011) has explained that obesity in the United States happens in the context of what she calls "cruel optimism", meaning the desire for something that actually precludes your well-being. In that vein, she regards obesity and desire for food as a sort of slow death. For Berlant, desire is a cluster of promises, and it is a cruel optimism when those promises are far from being achieved or achieved in excess and so become dangerous. In cases of repeated overeating the proto-states occur so frequently that craving becomes constant, resulting in a stable formation of desire rather than a plastic one. Oversupply of food does not necessarily trigger cravings; it might provoke other sensations, such as disgust. It is precisely because agency in the assemblage is distributed that social configurations are not the necessary causes of subjective events, but instead they work as conditions of possibilities for the development of tendencies and propensities for the subjects (Lara et al., 2017). In the US context, it is useful to remember Bennett's claim that "we can call the assemblage formed by these human and nonhuman bodies 'American consumption' and name as one of its effects the 'crisis of obesity'" (2010, 39).

It is in this context, where people are constantly stimulated by thousands of smells (and a lot of other triggers), that they are going to find themselves in a situation of having to "decide" what to do with their cravings. Meanwhile, an oversupply of food is going to modulate human bodies. As a result people may not have the desired agency to exercise will against the agency of matter, brain, and environment. In the field of nutritional epigenetics, food is starting to be understood as information, such that there is a shift away from its biomedical meaning as a fuel or substrate. Instead of providing stuff to burn, in the information model, food plays a role in the construction of the metabolic system itself: It acts to set up metabolic systems at the outset (Landecker, 2011). Of course, environmental conditions do not affect everybody in the same way. Analysis regarding the particularities of class, gender, and race have clearly shown that the right to choose – the right to neoliberal exercise of free will – is not equally distributed when it comes to food access or consumption management (see Probyn, 2009; Berlant, 2011; Guthman, 2011; Julier, 2013). It is precisely such inequality that makes it pertinent to look for alternative conscious strategies in a social configuration where not everyone can choose what to eat or crave.

As a food presented mostly in its sweet and solid version, chocolate partakes of the controversy around glucose and its effects in the body related to diabetes and numerous metabolic disorders (see O'Connell, 2011). Notwithstanding, this has not always been the case. Coe and Coe (2013) trace the history of chocolate from the Aztecs' drink of the gods all the way to the foundation of The Chocolate Society in UK and the blooming of chocolatier factories all around the world, especially in New York. As these authors explain, chocolate has recently become a sweet and solid food widely spread and easily accessible. Capitalistic industrialization of chocolate has resulted in the commercialization of low-quality chocolate high in sugar, containing less than 40% cacao solids, solid vegetable fat, and powdered milk. As Chantal Coady, owner of Rococo Chocolates and head of The Chocolate Society, has noted about so-called chocoholics: "These dietary villains . . . are responsible for chocolate's undeserved reputation as a fattening, tooth-rotting, addictive indulgence" (Coe and Coe, 2013, 260).

It is after these environmental conditions that smell molecules and brain proto-states inaugurate the process of change in the course of action. Chocolate craving then is an affective assemblage resulting from an emergent particular configuration of a set of agents. A craving is a bodily snapshot that maps a moment of connection of elements related to food. As Deleuze and Guattari put it, "Affects are precisely these non-human becomings of man [sic]" (1994, 169). An assemblage of desire "is never either a 'natural' or 'spontaneous' determination . . . but [is] always historically attributable. . . . [D]esire circulates in this agencement of heterogeneous elements, in this type of 'symbiosis'" (Deleuze, 1997, 185). If the concept of assemblage is welcome to affect studies, it is mainly because these environmental-organic configurations bypass conscious awareness of the body's capacities to affect and be affected. It follows that any intentionality manifested in the craving emerges as a complex entanglement between conscious and preconscious activity. The conscious deliberation, the moment of decision-making, appears as the last consequence emerging from our assemblage. As Luciana Parisi puts it, "[T]he subject is an appendix to the machine in desire, an accessory that does not determine ethical relations but only positions of will" (2004, 38).

Ruptures and continuities

As I walk away from the chocolate store, I continue to eat my tangy, dark chocolate, one bite after another as the world disappears throughout the clove and anise notes in my mouth. This chocolate is driving me crazy. Suddenly, I note that it is almost finished. Then I stop. An awkward combination of guilt and remorse infringe upon my mind. Only now do I remember that I'm trying to lose weight and that I need to control the calories I eat, or so my dietician and this guy from the gym say. But chocolate is so good. It is as if body and mind were on different sides, working for different purposes. The guilt gets worse as I remember that this is not the first time that I have indulged my cravings. I keep walking, thinking, and somehow knowing that the spicy powder for the drinkable chocolate is still in my bag, and the air temperature is decreasing.

For Deleuze and Guattari the production of desire in an assemblage occurs in the middle of two different forms of organization of encounters called molar and molecular strata.[4] Molecular strata correspond to those encounters that happen without following a previously defined, specific direction; rather the direction exclusively emerges from the interaction between properties and capacities of the agents at stake. Like the interaction between chocolate molecules and molecule receptors in my chocolate craving, the elements of this encounter do just what they can do: lock and unlock according to their shapes. These kinds of encounters produce unexpected new relations between the agencies, a "rupture" with the prior organization of agencies: like a molecule changing its disposition. Molar strata refer to other encounters within the assemblage that might be following a specific course of action determined at a distance by other forces, nonlocal agents of the assemblage delimitating the organization of the local elements, just as the encounter between my conscious self and the quasi-finished bar of chocolate is mediated by dietician discourses. These kinds of encounters work to reproduce certain kind of relations between the agencies, a "continuity" of certain relations among the agencies.

For the organism, the sensation of craving can be molar formations, especially when it is repeatedly induced by social forces arranging the configuration of the environment. Assemblage formations can make the body do things, and it can also trigger tendencies in our subjective events. Not everybody craves or even likes chocolate, but in Brooklyn, the distribution and diversification of chocolate practices increases the possibility to be attracted to and crave them. From the one-dollar little bar in the subway stall to the international variety in the street delis, from drinkable chocolate in cafés to the sophisticated and expensive chocolatiers factories, from organic-vegan stores for desserts to all ethnic forms of chocolate like Jewish bakeries, Latino drinkable, tamales, Japanese *wagashi*, and so on – a chocolate assemblage has so many nodes for you to connect to and thereby create a stable, recurrent desire, bringing your brain-body into multiple modes of attention, whereas your conscious agenda remains to restrict your pleasure. For instance, a particular chocolate cartography sets free an unexpected smell that redirects the organization of the body. A body knows it is chocolate and wants to perpetuate the organization of the proto-state. A body wants to continue the pleasure. However, for the cultural norms and alleged discipline that the conscious subject is pursuing, such a craving sensation represents a molecularity: a rupture with, for example, the regime of three meals per day to be healthy. Thus, consciousness tries to break desire to control the course of action, to conform to what is socially expected for the body. We can say then that conscious control expected in the experience of craving is a form of molar use of conscious capacities.

As Massumi explains, in molar strata "powerful forces descend to assure that what the body wills is, on average, what 'society' wills for it" (1992, 75). But, if the game between molar and molecular strata of organization is about ruptures and continuities in the kind of relations among the elements of the assemblage, then we can assume that molarization should work in such a rhythm that a molecular line of escape is always possible. Moreover, it is a tendency toward a different rhythm: "[T]he stronger the molar organization is, the more it induces a molecularization of its own elements, relations, and elementary apparatuses" (Deleuze and Guattari, 1987, 215). This means that the restrictive character of the relations among certain elements of the assemblage are prone to be interrupted. For example, the more restrictive the diet is and the more it tries to resist cravings, the more people are likely to indulge their cravings. The tension between molar and molecular is a constant one, as Massumi explains: "No body can really be molar. Bodies are made molar, with varying degrees of success" (1992, 64). As Delanda (2016) explains, molar and molecular are not mutually exclusive binary categories but rather phases of the same process that can be transformed into one another and even coexist as mixtures.

Conscious activity acquires molar status just when it is committed to restrict pleasure. Let us not forget that for Deleuze, consciousness needs a cause; in the Spinozist vein he argues that desire is an "appetite together with consciousness of the appetite. But he [Spinoza] specifies that this is only a nominal definition of desire. . . . [W]e need then to arrive at a real definition of desire, one that at the same time shows the 'cause' by which consciousness is hollowed out, as it were, in the appetitive process" (Deleuze, 1988, 20–21). What is at stake in a chocolate craving within the social configuration described is an assemblage in which consciousness has been given the "cause" of control device, and it emerges in this form within the production of desire. Elsewhere Deleuze has argued that "pleasure seems to me to interrupt the immanent process of desire; pleasure seems to me to be on the side of strata and organization" (1997, 189). So, it is pleasure, not restrictive control, that has the capacity to rearrange the role of consciousness within the assemblage. Deleuze's assemblage theory provides a system in which consciousness can be analyzed in terms of the strata from which it is being organized as a component of desire production. The capacity of conscious to receive directions and the organizational capacities of pleasure point to the necessary rethinking of the sovereign and restrictive capacities of consciousness in current neoliberalism.

Craving shows us how organisms are organized beyond mere biological evolutional criteria, organisms, cells, and neurons, and its activity has been acculturated. Cravings are relatively new forms of desire, aesthetic desires, as Gard (2009) would say. Cravings have been with us throughout history, even contributing to changes in food consumption, snacks, and appetizers, and cultural rituals are a good example of that. The French "*apéritif*", Chilean "*once*", American "snacking", even the Mexican "*antojitos*" that literally means "little cravings" are all examples of culturally established rituals more related to aesthetic desires than to the need for food. They are established and ritualized molecular investments into the molar aggregate, the rupture of desire producing a cultural continuity. Given this cultural and historical organization of desiring production, we have to notice, as Damasio (2010) puts it, that what is meant by conscious deliberation has little to do with the ability to control actions in the moment and everything to do with the ability to plan ahead and decide which actions we want or do not want to carry out. Conscious deliberation is largely about decisions taken over extended periods of time, as much as days or weeks in the case of some decisions. Rarely less than minutes, conscious deliberation is not about split-second decisions. In the case of feeling a craving, there is usually little time to "decide" or, better, to act with self-awareness and marshal self-control. You might recognize the craved food, but this acknowledgment is not yet a conscious activity as much as an automatic and "thoughtless" response. "Conscious deliberation is about reflection over knowledge" (Damasio, 2010, 287). It follows that such a temporality of mind is more prone to be committed to forms of organization proper to its own temporality. This means, for conscious activity, it is easier to engage – to rationally understand – and deal with arguments about how the body should be, like socially desirable standards of the body. When diet advisors suggest avoiding consumption, their position is "just say no." As Damasio (2010) sees it,

> [T]his strategy may be adequate when one has to preempt an innocuous finger movement, but not when one needs to stop an action urged by a strong desire or appetite, precisely the kind posed by any addiction to drugs, alcohol, attractive foods, or sex. Successful not-saying requires a lengthy conscious preparation". (288–289)

Consciousness and pre-conscious activity work in different rhythms. This is why you can't apply conscious resources to preconscious battles, at least not as straightforwardly as has been assumed. The strategy must be more sophisticated than that. The management of desire cannot be reduced to the restrictive capacity of consciousness or the possibility of applying it during the event of the craving, especially knowing that conscious molarization represents an alienation from other forces that are not precisely our own. We ought to consider opportunities for consciousness to operate within the possibilities of its own rhythm and in better attunement with one's own body. In other words, individual conscious management of desire must depart from a diversification of the function of conscious. Consciousness is capable of managing important decisions for long periods of time. But the fact of the spontaneous desire for food reveals the need for strategies of conscious management that respond to the eventness: the time when the nonconscious drivers are in command.

Pleasure and plasticity

The chocolate store I always pass by offers a huge variety of products. Nonetheless, ever since I moved to Brooklyn, I normally get the same tangy one and the same spicy drinkable: These are my favorites. But my chocolate cravings are making a diet a complicated experience more, I think, due to the emotional consequences than the actual pounds that I am – or that I am not – losing. Indulgence feels good but only as it lasts. Right after comes guilt. As I stir the drinkable chocolate with a wood spoon, I'm wishing that the fugitive pleasure that comes with it would last forever. I wish chocolate pleasure was not followed by guilt.

Following Spinoza, Deleuze (1988) explains that for the encounters within an assemblage, the capacity of things might be increased (good passion) or decreased (bad passion). It must be noted that when human consciousness is participating in an encounter, the effect of such an encounter depends on one's susceptibility to be distance driven for the continuity of nonlocal purposes. Human consciousness might be thinking ideas that are not our own and thus working under a molar regime of activity. In terms of chocolate craving, if we please the craving without modifying anything in the way we eat it, indulgence will feel restrictive to our capacity to control and regulate our eating habits, taking power away from us. On the one hand, chocolate can make you feel guilty and frustrated if the project of consciousness is that of restricting pleasure. On the other hand, if we indulge our cravings but invest in producing pleasure out of such an indulgence, then power is being added to our capacities, meaning increasing the capacity for pleasure.

The body-brain is exposed to the oversupply of food, lots of chocolate stores, and products everywhere triggering cravings, but it is also exposed to health and beauty discourses about the body, like when my dietician suggested to me that I lose weight. The body-mind component of the assemblage is called on to invest in different capacities simultaneously: restrictive capacities on one hand, capacities for pleasure on the other. But consciousness can engage with a different project, and in doing so, it can modify the experience of the craving, even its biological and preconscious elements. Catherine Malabou (2008, 2012, 2015) has suggested the term "neuroplasticity" to refer to the brain's ability to biologically change and be changed.[5] In a general sense, she suggests that "awakening a conscious of the brain . . . means awakening a conscious of the self, a consciousness of consciousness, if you will, which is also to say a comprehension of the transition from the neuronal to the mental, a comprehension of cerebral change" (2008, 66). Malabou's idea of an appropriation of the material plasticity of the brain resonates in what Schwartz and Bagley (2002) refer to as "self-directed plasticity", meaning that might it be more related to a sort of functional or synaptic plasticity caused by learning and cognitive activity. For Malabou, "If neuronal function is an event or should bring about events, this is so precisely because it is itself able to create events, to eventualize the program and thus, in a certain sense, to deprogram it" (2008, 8). Such potential to create new forms of consciousness carries the political ambivalence of emancipation and control (Bhardar and Goldberg-Hiller, 2015), but at the very least offers the possibility of diversifying conscious commitments to include the concerns of the body. The idea of consciously provoked brain plasticity to deprogram brain activity can be applied to the modification of the experience of cravings. And this idea represents an actual different way to use consciousness in the management of desire for food: the use of consciousness informed by its possibilities and attuned to the timing of the event of desire. Following Malabou's plastic vein, Sparrow has recently proposed aesthetic pleasure as the key to reach the plastic condition of human bodies. In what he calls his "principle of aesthetic individuation", Sparrow suggests, "since a body's sensory identity is determined by the sensory blueprint of its environment, that body's power to affect and be affected will only be as complex as the totality of its aesthetic experiences" (2015, 216).

Pleasure must be made. Consciousness deploys resources, like its capacity to focus, that can be used to intensify the aesthetic properties of the matter. When eating chocolate, for example, the affective sensation of chocolate properties throughout the body can be intensified by virtue of our conscious focus on it. The affective sensation of chocolate's properties throughout the body can be intensified by our conscious focus on it. Attention must be given to all the playful properties of the food such as smell, colors, temperature, sound, texture, aftertaste, how it makes your belly feel, the energy you are absorbing, and so on. Mol encourages such attention to flavor when she claims "The very act of attending to what you eat . . . should increase your appreciation. More strongly still, it should increase your ability to appreciate" (Mol, 2013a, 101). Focusing on the sweetness of chocolate, for example, is not going to make it sweeter, but it will give the body more information about its sweetness. The body will be more aware. If we get to experience the intensification of the properties of the food through a pleasurable experience, we are able to modify the state that the body produces when it gets in touch with such a substance. What is more, pleasure has the potential to rearrange the way in which body-brain is affected and participates in the whole assemblage.

For the body to maintain a suppleness of composition, Sparrow suggests, "[I]t must actively expose itself to percepts and affects that intensify its power by bolstering its tolerance, that enable it to radiate new sensations and pleasurable affects" (Sparrow, 2015, 230); so we should work on the productions of our own pleasure. The modification of brain formation by altering the history of brain encounters is what Malabou recognizes as "the second field of plasticity", defined as "the modification of neuronal connections by means of the modulation of synaptic efficacy." It is at this level, she says "that plasticity imposes itself with the greatest clarity and force in 'opening' its meaning" (Malabou, 2008, 21). A relation to certain food might be rigidly mapped, the kind of food we always crave and in exactly the same way, maybe under the same circumstances, maybe from the same store, just like my favorite chocolates. These kinds of stable relations trigger molarized components of the assemblage of desire; the body has learned a state and keeps reproducing it. Influenced by the social configuration of the assemblage, the brain-body can develop well-defined molar structures, but this kind of craving needs to be molecularized. To do that, we must generate an aesthetic consumption, a creative one centered on pleasure that could always be different. An aesthetics of pleasure, as a molecular device to generate plasticity, is our main conscious resource for diversifying the production of desire toward a better regulation of food consumption. As Bhandar and Goldberg-Hiller suggests, plasticity is "an agency of disobedience to every constituted form, a refusal to submit to a model" (2015, 9). The disobedient quality of pleasure production in the event of a craving relies on a simple gesture: a more consciously produced desire now replacing distance-driven desire production, moving from a desire as something that is being done to us (and to our brain) to something we are doing using the resource of our conscious brain.

One must be careful here; bringing in self-directed brain plasticity to claim its potential to diversify experience doesn't mean gaining sovereignty, at least not as a capacity to control. It means rather the possibility for a degree of freedom that understands the lack of such sovereignty, freedom beyond sovereignty as Krause (2015) would have it. The argument is not that through brain plasticity we would have more efficient control over ourselves; it is rather the claim that we might gain awareness about the impossibility of such control. We might gain accurate consciousness of what can we do with our brains by understanding what can be done to them by the assemblage and, particularly, by the molar forces playing within assemblage of desire production. The capacities of the body, including the brain, can't be fully managed by ourselves. Self-directed brain plasticity doesn't mean a synaptic self taking over; it is rather a conscious subject knowing the limits and therefore the potentialities of brain consciousness. The environment has "some" power upon our brains and can do "certain" things to it – so can we. A subject whose only conscious resources are applied "against" desire production in forms of restrictive capacity, or "in favor" of pleasing desire by overeating, are the kind of subjects resulting from the assemblages arranged by capitalism and involving the capture of some cognitive and neuronal capacities – like attention. This sort of assemblage is what Sampson (2017) has called "neurocapitalism", featured by brain-directed arrangements that affect brain capacities.

Instead of encouraging fast conscious deliberation, focusing attention requires slowing ourselves down. We usually don't take the time to do this; we eat too fast, with too little attention in such a way that we are unaware of food properties. Environmental distribution of food contributes to the absence of pleasure in the moment of eating. As some scholars have pointed out, eating practices are commonly related to anxiety (Probyn, 2000; Lara, 2015b), stress (Berlant, 2011), or guilt (Mol, 2013a). Pleasure is not something that the socio-cultural environment encourages in our relationship with food, at least not thoughtful pleasure. Pleasure must not be confused with other experiences like satisfaction produced by overeating or pleasure associated with only certain kinds of (generally fast-food) products. These kinds of sensations have certainly been promoted by capitalism. Again, pleasure has to be made.

The idea of eating slowly and pleasurably requires some clarifications; a lot has been said in relation to the class, racial, and gendered blindness of this kind of discourse (see Berlant, 2011; Guthman, 2011;

Julier, 2013). Also, how perspectives suggesting any sort of individual action, like creating pleasure, might exclude those who, because of their socioeconomic conditions, do not have the necessary resources to attain this kind of pleasure. In Guthman's words, these perspectives "lead to a disproportionate focus on individual consumption choices about which people should be educated rather than, say, a focus on enacting policies that would enforce corporate accountability, or in mitigating the consequences for those most harmed" (2011, 8). Well, the answer to this sort of critique is rather a straightforward one: Slowing down and creating pleasure cannot possibly constitute a politics of eating in a general sense. If it all was about individual choices, it would be a neoliberal politics of self-regulation neglecting social configurations and other political forces participating in desire production. Food's inequality is not a matter of personal responsibility but a social one. This chapter is by no means trying to propose a general solution to all contingencies within the assemblage; the aim here is much more modest: to explore the possibilities of human consciousness in the moment of the event, especially given the social configuration that escapes full individual control and distributes agency unequally among subjects. In other words, creating pleasure will never modify the whole assemblage of desiring production, but it might diversify the role of human consciousness within it.

In a general sense, this chapter is exploring the resource of pleasure production as a plastic-organic device for political disobedience beyond the control-centered alternatives of desire repression to challenge the traditional way in which molecular and organic scales interact when it comes to eating practices. Such an approach might be useful given stable and problematic expressions of the assemblage as molar cravings, like a recurrent chocolate craving producing guilt. My approach to the event of a craving has required us to consider craving through the notion of assemblage, to be aware of the heterogeneity involved in the relatedness of the event of the assemblage, and then to understand that conscious activity is not the center and, so, cannot fully exercise control over the other components of the assemblage. In addition to this, there is always the possibility that some components of the assemblage act at a distance to propitiate ruptures and continuities among the relations of the elements within assemblages. It is crucial to understand that the human mind might be embedded in molar regimes or activity, subjected to other agencies like discourses about health and about how our relation to pleasure should be. Conscious capacities might just as well be restricted by environmental conditions of food. Understanding that the molar and molecular strata of organization are pulling and pushing within the assemblage opens the possibility to think about a different usage of consciousness in our desire for food. I have offered the idea of pleasure as a consciously driven device to produce brain plasticity and to diversify the production of desire. This provides the body with the possibility of a broader spectrum of desire to be evoked in the future and, at the same time, represents a nonrestrictive use of conscious deliberation. This essay is not about resisting cravings but about diversifying them.

Notes

1 For discussion on the advantages and disadvantages on the arrival of neurosciences to affect studies and social sciences in general, see Connolly Neuropolitics (2002) and Papoulias and Callard (2010), "Biology's Gift", *Body & Society, 16*(1), pp. 29–56. For Deleuze and Guattari's warning on the brain as a relational device embedded in human experience, see Deleuze and Guattari (1994, 209).

2 There are two main theories on how smell receptors and odor molecules interact: shape and vibration theories. Whereas the debate is currently unsolved in molecular biology, in this chapter and I will follow Shepherd's take on "shape" to offer an account of the chocolate interaction. Henshaw has suggested that the problem with shape theory is "it requires a unique 'lock' (receptor) in the nose for each unique 'key' (odorant) that humans can perceive. Since it is generally accepted that a person can distinguish up to about 10, 000 different odors, that would require a lot of receptors in the nose. The number of unique smell receptors is believed to be far less than this – perhaps around 350" (2012, 41). For a general explanation on those two theories of de-codification of smell molecules, see Henshaw, 2012, Chapter 2, on chemical stimuli. For an in-depth explanation on the shape-versus-vibration debate, see Luca Turin (2007).

3 The term was originally proposed by Rizzolatti and Craighero (2004). For a review of the critiques to mirror neuron theory, particularly for its inattention to the cultural context in which bodily simulation occurs, see Pitts-Taylor (2013); Leys (2011); Martin (2010). For the Deleuze and Guattari warning on the brain as a relational device embedded in human experience, see Deleuze and Guattari (1994, 209); see also Deleuze (1988). For a discussion on the advantages and cautions of the arrival of neurosciences to affect studies and social sciences in general, see Connolly (2002); Papoulias and Callard (2010), Fitzgerald and Callard (2014), and Cromby et al. (2011).

4 Brian Massumi explains the molar/molecular strata, arguing that such a distinction "*has nothing whatsoever to do with scale*. Molecular and molar do not correspond to 'small' and 'large', 'part' and 'whole', 'organ' and 'organism', 'individual' and 'society'. There are molarities of every magnitude (the smallest being the nucleus of the atom). The distinction is not one of scale, but of mode of composition: it is qualitative, not quantitative" (1992, 54–55, his italics)

5 In her review of the literature of neuroscience Malabou recognizes at least three different forms of brain plasticity: developmental, modulational, and reparative. For Malabou (2008) developmental plasticity refers to the morphological and

structural modifications the brain goes through in the developmental process. Modulational plasticity is about the changes in neuronal connections resulting from one's relation with the environment, as in learning processes of cognitive activity. Reparative plasticity refers to the brain's capacity to heal and recover from trauma or lessons. For a review of the literature on neuronal plasticity, see Pitts-Taylor (2016), particularly Chapter 1.

4 Wine and time

This chapter works as a wine tasting;[1]
three moments will bring different information:
The first one, the perspective,
requires you to take some distance,
to make an appreciation within a broad context.
You see; you smell. You get our departure point.
Once you are inside each other comes the mouthfeel,
a second moment that will tell about its textures and flavors.
You taste; you feel. You get attuned with our rhythms.
That is the moment you'll get the wine. In the third moment,
the aftertaste, you will enjoy the sweet spices.
You swallow; you breathe. Then you get the perception,
and a promise of returning will be diffracted in your mind.
For the best pairing use this soundtrack:[2]
www.youtube.com/watch?v=g5QL6D3qs20.

Perspective: a longer project of time

It was April 6, 1922. Paris. The atmosphere was strange. The colors had a suspicious brightness, and the smells of discord were expanding and ready to keep wafting for a long while. Spring was about to get turbulent: The Societe´ Francaise de Philosophie was hosting a debate between Henri Bergson and Albert Einstein – the subject: time and the special theory of relativity. It has been argued that it was rather a competition between physics and philosophy to see which one could speak for the nature of time and about which of these two disciplines would have the last word (Canales, 2015). Bergson wanted to claim that "all did not end" with relativity. He was clear: "[O]nce we[3] admit the Theory of Relativity as a physical theory, all is not finished." Philosophy, he modestly argued, still had a place. Einstein disagreed. He fought against giving philosophy (and by inference Bergson) any role in matters of time. His objections were based on his views about the role of philosophy in society – views that differed from Bergson's (Canales, 2005, 1170). Certainly, there was no wine or attunement on that day, not yet. Much has been said about that debate: "Einstein didn't listen to Bergson" (Latour, 2011); "Bergson doesn't understand relativity theory" (Einstein, 1987); "the historical origins of the Science Wars lay in Einstein's and Bergson's fateful meeting" (Sokal and Bricmont, 1998). Canales (2015) has signaled how in several texts thereafter, Bergson attempted to explain what had not been understood in the debate. In fact, following the spirit of clarification rather than confrontation, in the introduction of the translation to English of "Simultaneity and Duration" (Bergson, 1965),[4] Dingle suggested that they were in complete agreement:

> The only absolute simultaneity, according to both, was that of the events at the same place, and it was a basic requirement of Einstein's theory – and the most striking evidence of his insight – that the simultaneity of separated events could be only a matter of voluntary definition. There was no difference at all here between them except that, owing to their different point of view, Bergson stressed the intuitive simultaneity of coincident events and Einstein the learned simultaneity of separated events. They were simply calling attention to different sides of the same coin.
>
> (Dingle, 1965, xxxvi)

The reminiscences of the debate between Bergson and Einstein still resonate almost 100 years later. It has changed the way we produce knowledge about time, among other ways, because of its political implications, like the split between the sciences and philosophy in which the legitimacy of the production of knowledge being attributed to the former is usually to the detriment of the latter (Canales, 2015). After this debate, the role of philosophy was taken to be a subjective position that didn't add to the scientific understanding of time. By consequence, according to Einstein, the role of the human being and philosophy were relegated to a passive and inaccurate perception of a phenomenon, time, only understood by physics. Time is of great importance to grasp not just human life but a large scope of processes involved in reality that capture the attention of philosophy, science, art, media studies, and social theories in general. But if time has once been the pretext to hinder and discredit the relation between science and philosophy, time itself is also the "space" where these matrixes of production of knowledge found each other again but this time in light of contemporary studies of affect.

From their beginnings, affect studies and the so-called affective turn emerged – although not explicitly – as what we can call a project of recognition of multiple temporalities simultaneously participating in human experience as well as a project of locating and relating multiple temporalities within the body such as a frame for affect.[5] Usually these different temporalities were associated with differences in speed corresponding to conscious and nonconscious activity (Angerer et al., 2014). One of the main resources that has allowed affect studies to recognize such multiple temporalities operating in different scales of reality is the re-encounters with some expressions of sciences like neurosciences, molecular biology, and quantum physics, among others (see Clough, 2008; Blackman and Venn, 2010; Lara and Enciso, 2014) as a sort of reparative gesture, healing what was once broken. Yet, healing even more, the second resource of affect theory – that has allowed both the re-encounter with science and the understanding of time – has been precisely Bergson's philosophy.

Bergson's ideas were first brought to affect studies by theorists like Keith Ansell-Pearson (2001), Grosz (2004), and Hansen (2006). The contributions of these authors expanded and deepened the Deleuzian tradition in affect studies usually attributed to Massumi (2002). In doing so, we had to acknowledge that some of the ideas that are fundamental for Deleuze came directly from Bergson's philosophy, such as that of the distinction between the actual and the virtual. After all, Deleuze declared himself a Bergsonian (Deleuze, 2011). Bergson's philosophy was crucial to establish affect studies as centered in the body and as what we are referring to now as a longer project of time. However, after Deleuze and Bergson, the contemporary landscape in affect studies seems to be seduced by another philosopher – Whitehead – whom also had a Bergsonian understanding of time.[6] We can witness the Whiteheadian trend in recent contributions like those by Parisi (2013), Stenner and Greco (2013); Manning and Massumi (2014), or Hansen (2015). Deleuze, Bergson, and Whitehead shared in common a nonessentialist philosophical project – with Spinozist roots – that has been labeled as "process philosophies" and that so far has worked as the main philosophical frame for affect studies (Lara, 2015). This recent turn of affect studies toward Whitehead's philosophy may be attributed to what Shaviro (2014a) explains as a convergence of interests and commitments among Whitehead's philosophy, speculative realism (Bryant et al., 2011), and new materialism (Barad, 2007; Bennett, 2010; Coole and Frost, 2010). We would include in that convergence the quite closely related OOO (Meillassoux, 2008; Harman, 2016; Morton, 2016) and nonhuman studies (Grusin, 2015). All these trending lines of thought are affecting and being affected by the consolidated field of affect studies.

Although new Whitehedian lines of thought are extremely useful to further advance the theorization of affect and its complex interweaving with life itself, at the other side of affect studies, there are still certain critiques that insist on claiming a lack of empirical analysis (Leys, 2011; Wetherell, 2012) as well as what Blackman sees as a "rush to dismiss subjectivity (that) seems premature" (2014, 9. 373, our parenthesis). Although we may agree, we also think that such a turn back to the study of social interaction cannot happen in the same way that hitherto has been used by social sciences through the twentieth century: the study of human interactions centered in language or exclusively through an empirical (and registrable) interaction of a conscious level of activity among organisms (see Enciso and Lara, 2014). These may be available resources, but they do not suffice as a standalone solution. We cannot deny the importance of language and concrete human interactions, but if we are to include "social practices" in the study of affect, we should use concepts that help us include those practices while also helping unfold the other scales of the reality entangled in human experience. It is precisely to that purpose that we still need Bergson's philosophy. Here, we are proposing to use his notion of duration because it invites us to recognize the multiple rhythms and temporalities connected in the event. The concept of duration still complements the most sophisticated Whiteheadian advances in current affect studies. Duration is particularly relevant for a study of the perception of time committed to affect studies because it allows us to focus on subjective experience by exploring material relations. At the same time, critiques of affect studies are right: Human experience and interaction must be addressed. But they are also wrong: We cannot do it without unfolding other scales of reality and their temporalities at stake in affective processes. In that sense, this longer project of time doesn't root itself in the past. It is more about imagining the future through speculation, as Vannini (2015) would suggest.

For Bergson, duration is a qualitative multiplicity, "a succession of qualitative changes, which melt into and permeate one another, without precise outlines, without any tendency to externalize themselves in relation to one another, without any affiliation with a number" (Bergson, 2001, 104). Time as well as duration is not measurable or quantifiable;

it is rather an "organic evolution . . . a pure heterogeneity within which there are no distinct qualities" (Bergson, 2001, 226).

For Bergson, everybody – whether human, object, or other – has its own duration, meaning its own patterns of temporality. Each body's duration contains and unfolds other durations, such as the processes inside the human body following their own rhythms, such as of digestion, blood circulation, or breathing. That is, duration always involves the simultaneity of flows of temporalities expressed as material events being connected with each other. Thus, Bergsonian duration puts on the table the problem of spatialization of time (see Bergson, 2001, Chapter 2; Keith Ansell-Pearson, 2001, especially Chapter 1). For Bergson, when two bodies are in the same physical space, their duration is simultaneous because they both depend on the duration of a like third, our own; "this duration is ours only when our consciousness is concerned with us alone, but it becomes equally theirs when our attention embraces the three flows in a single indivisible act" (Bergson, 1965, 52). Then, implicit in this duration is what Deleuze identified as a "fundamental triplicity of fluxes" (2011, 80).

In other words, Bergsonian duration emerges when bodies get together, at least three of them. Yet, the only duration involved in simultaneity is that of the present (Bergson, 2001), the duration of the moment that connects our three bodies. But even if bodies are together, their temporality is not always easy to register, if we consider that some of these bodies may be apparently inner objects like glass or cork. For Bergson, vibration in the molecular level is what provides duration to all objects; hence vibration is the essential link between the activity of the matter and the multiple rhythms of duration. As Bergson notes, matter "resolves itself into numberless vibrations, all linked together in uninterrupted continuity, all bound up with each other, and traveling in every direction like shivers through an immense body" (2005, 208).

It must be noted that those affect studies addressing the vibrational quality of the matter have been in one way or another also concerned by time and commonly interested in affective properties of sound. We can find such an intersection in the vibrational ontology of Goodman (2010); contributions about politics of affect and sound (Thompson and Biddle, 2013); studies addressing different temporalities in relation with media and art (Angerer et al., 2014), or these can be explicitly centered in rhythm and movement (Henriques et al., 2014) as well as the importance of rhythm for "affective synchronization" (Bösel, 2014). All these contributions address in one way or another what Clough calls "rhythm affect"; as she suggested, affect "is an event of dead time seething with vibrations, with rhythms ready for propagation or infection" (2010, 228). As Bergson knew, and as we know also from the new materialists, in the quantum field everything is vibrating (Barad, 2007). But, how can we consciously register the effects of the vibration of matter? And even more, what does it tell us about psychological processes like perception?

In the case discussed by Bergson and Einstein in 1922, the triplicity at stake was that of the so-called twin paradox, which includes one "observer" (a physicist) and two clocks, each of which was held by one of two twin brothers. One of them went into space; the other one remained on Earth.[7] Well, we have chosen our own three elements to enhance the fundamental triplicity to provide an everyday human interaction as a scenario for theorizing the material basis of the perception of time. Here there is no one human "observer", but one kind of red wine, and not two clocks, but two human bodies. Nobody is going into space; our bodies are hanging out, drinking wine, and time will happen. Having wine as the "point of reference" will help us understand the crucial role of matter in the emergence of time, especially if what interests us about time is the way it comes to human experience or what has been addressed in psychology as perception.

Bergson and Einstein's debate on time seems to be a good frame to point out that the study of some classical objects of interest for psychology – such as perception – shouldn't be isolated from debates concerning science and philosophy, especially as they now intersect within affect studies. But let's save "perception" for later. As we will argue in this piece, once illuminated by the light of the contributions from affect studies, time also appears as a promising "space" for a new project of exploration of subjectivity and mental process largely owned by psychology. This is our departure point. As in a wine tasting, you have to start by stepping back to recognize the substance that you are about to taste in light of the broader context, to then appreciate the colors, to feel the smells, and to recognize elements coming from far in time and space – like grapes, distant lands, or old debates. Take one step back as a gesture of anticipation; thus, distance becomes time, and we can see the past. We need that to locate additional information, to tempt imagination, and to see where we are coming from. We have not even started. Don't have expectations; don't perceive; just taste. This is about to get tasty.

Mouthfeel: attunement and diffraction

Breathe in; breathe out. Cheers. Take another sip, and we smile. We drink at the same time; the waves of wine are dragging us to each other's feelings. But we won't drown, so we breathe to bring a little of ourselves in the waves, and the rhythm of our breathing synchronizes like a secret pact. Breathe in; breathe out. We look at the wine and look back to each other; our movements seem like a well thought-out choreography but are just the aesthetics of the encounter. There are words being said, but we miss them through the sound of wine falling into the glass. The note of sweetness from her voice makes the air vibrate; it even resonates in the aftertaste of the last sip; it meets the cinnamon and the oaks. We smell it again; it has changed. Breathe in; breathe out once more and for the first time again. The moment is breathing as well; so is the wine. It brings flashbacks from its past, maybe a reminiscence of another weather, warm and cozy, like this moment. Here it is winter, but it feels otherwise: the blowing breeze of the Californian summer where we have never been together until now. Perhaps it is the wine that happens. Perhaps we happen to the wine. Breathe in; breathe out. The brightness of the color comes into our own gaze; it becomes our own gaze. The silky texture caresses our tongues. Silkiness is infecting her smile, and her smile echoes all over the room. We are now embedded in an uncanny atmosphere: another space, another time, another us. Let's see if we can come back. But no hurry – there is time for another sip. Cheers. Breathe in; breathe out.

That was the wine's time. The moment narrated in this field note is going to help us understand what material events participate in the perception of time when two people share a bottle of wine. To account for the perception of the time, we should focus, as Bergson would have suggested, on the temporalities mobilized by matter that create the basis for the event. In this second moment of the chapter, we are going to use this note on the experience of sharing a glass of wine to develop an approach to time perception based on the interaction of material events and human perception. To do so, we are going to consider events from two different scales of reality. First, we will consider and describe encounters between organisms – such as human bodies – to address the material events and their lapses of time. Specifically, we are going to introduce the concept of attunement. Next, we will include events from the molecular scale of reality, events occurring within the wine and accessed through our experience as reflected by the resource of aesthetic writing. This writing resource, we will see, could bring material events that were apparently not part of the event. To address those events in the molecular scale, we are going to introduce the concept of diffraction. Both of our concepts – attunement and diffraction – will help us consider the temporality of each event in relation to the temporality of the social event we analyze here: the sharing of a glass of wine. This means that attunement and diffraction are consistent with Bergsonian duration as a philosophical frame.

Perception of time, understood as a process with a material base, would be better referred to as the concatenation of material modifications of rhythm in different scales of activity. To the human body, it would be a sensation raising an affective temporality. As our wine's time suggests, such temporality could be shared by means of bodies sharing the same substance. Of course experience is never the same in different bodies due to the particularities of each organic architecture; however, taking in the same substance reduces the range of possibilities of unshared experience. The first concept for our analysis, organic attunement, is inspired by the "affective attunement" originally proposed by developmental psychologist Stern (2000).[8] Affective attunement was for Stern a concept that allowed him to systematize the observation of the relationship between human bodies (mother and baby). From the beginning, it was a resource for developing an ethology of organisms. In Stern's research, affective attunement is defined as a "performance of behaviors that express the quality of feeling of a shared affect state without imitating the exact behavioral expression of the inner state" (Stern, 2000, 142). Crucial for this notion of attunement is the replacement of understanding such matching in terms of imitation with the notion of attunement or the transmission of cross-modal qualities between bodies. For Stern, there are six specific "types of match", or the features of behavior that could be matched: 1) absolute intensity; 2) intensity contour; 3) temporal beat (a regular pulsation in time is matched); 4) rhythm (a pattern of pulsations of unequal stress is matched); 5) duration (the time span of the behavior is matched); and 6) shape. We can see how the notions linked to time (3, 4, and 5) are committed with observable behavior, but at the same time they are not begging for a linear notion of time. Rather, the temporality of the attunement could be thought of as centered on small events of encounters of different temporalities coming from different bodies. The duration of attunement fits with Bergson's duration as much as both involve certain qualities melting into each other along independent lapses.

Stern calls this sort of translation from one sensory modality to another "cross-modal transformation" (he addresses intensity, time, and shape), for example, loudness of sounds being translated into brightness of lights or "the note of sweetness from her voice" that "makes the air vibrate", as in our wine's time note. In the attunement, qualities of different natures are translated into different properties of the bodies, and this idea works also for nonhuman bodies. For example, the wine that has been fermented in barrels of oak is exposed to the porous quality and toastiness of the oak, which contributes to a reduction of oxygen that is translated into the texture of the wine, commonly resulting in a silky one – like the zinfandel – from the wine's time. But a different texture also affects the way the bouquet propagates in relation with the glass and the temperature of the room, and so on. As described in our wine's time note, "The silky texture caresses our tongues. Silkiness is infecting her smile, and her smile echoes all over the room." The cross-modal interchange of properties goes from wine to physiological sensations to the whole transformation of the atmosphere in the space of the event. What makes wine such a great substance to talk about attunement is its openness and sensitivity. Wine absorbs the features of the environment like light, temperature, and sound and translates them into its own molecular pattern of activity that is expressed in the wine's qualities and later brings these patterns inside our bodies. This relational essence is what sommeliers and oenologists refer to as the aliveness of wine.

Substances like wine do not passively wait to be grasped or perceived. Wine is actively interacting with us; our bodies are one of the elements wine experiences, as is the land, the glass, time, and so on. Human bodies are the ultimate substance of wine's trajectory. As Shaviro says, "[P]erception, feeling and aesthetics are universal structures, not specifically human ones" (Shaviro, 2014b, 61). Wine reconfigures its patterns of molecular activity in relation with the patterns of activity of the medium; that is, wine attunes to the rhythms of anything that touches it. It is embedded on "an intimate, compositional process of dwelling in spaces that bears, gestures, gestates, worlds" that Stewart has defined as atmospheric attunement (2011, 445). Wine creates its own atmosphere, and as Anderson explains, "[T]he atmosphere of an aesthetic object discloses the space – time of an 'expressedworld' – it does not represent objective space – time or lived space – time. It creates a space of intensity that overflows a represented world organized into subjects and objects or subjects and other subjects" (Anderson, 2009, 79; see also Anderson, 2014, Chapter six).

Changes in the patterns of activity appear in two scales of activity, the molecular and the organic; henceforth, they are translated not just in cross-modal transformation but also in a sort of cross-scalar way, like a molecular rhythm or pattern of activity being translated into a new organic pattern expressed within a larger scale, something that we can see, for example, somebody's cheeks becoming red when drinking wine or the brightness of the wine "becoming our own gaze" as in the wine's time. Under such a broader conception, "rhythm no longer belongs to a body as a quality or asset and it is not attached to anything other than itself. Rhythm may not emerge tied to a plane of action or to something else outside it, allowing instead for an (inter)action between different planes, or bodies" (Ikoniadou, 2014, 154). Rhythm is the main quality that propitiates the cross-modal transmission that is at stake in the attunement. This is close to Bergson's definition of affect as "that part or aspect of the inside of our body which we mix with the image of external bodies" (2005, 58).

In Stern's attunement, the cross-modal transmission of qualities dwells in the interaction between human bodies, as a form of expressionism, and testifies to the continuum of a range of events whose properties circulate between bodies. Stern's affective attunement, then, is also concerned with the different durations brought to the event of interaction between organic bodies. But the idea of attunement also allows us to direct attention to the eventness of sharing an experience and then to the duration, timing, and rhythm that are intimately connected with material properties, as Bergsonian philosophy has long elucidated. Yet, Stern's "affective attunement" still must be expanded to the molecular and quantum scales by the possibilities of its own principal: patterns of movements being materiality transmitted. If movement and aliveness are to be recognized as a shared property of all the bodies, then matter itself generates its own rhythmical organization by means of its vibrational movements. It is here where we propose to consider a perspective that may address the organization in different scales of a reality achieved by virtue of the contact and the transmission of rhythmical patterns of activity. Following Ikaniadou, if vibration is an immanent way of relationality of all matters, then it should be conceptualized "as a living form/force rather than a metric one" (2014, 150).

Bergson was well aware of this immanence of movement, even when it may not be empirically recognizable; he asserted: "I hold then the two ends of the chain, muscular sensation within me, the sensible qualities of matter without me, and neither in the one case nor in the other do I see movement, if there be movement, as a mere relation: it is an absolute" (Bergson, 2005, 196). Bergsonian duration was from the beginning meant to be understood beyond human interaction because it involves an auto-determined lapse of time able to "store up, in a given interval, as great a number of phenomena as we please" (Bergson, 2005, 205); thus countless agents will interact in one single moment, even when they are apparently not present. So, due to its metaphysical character, the notion of duration may find "scientific" support more accurately with quantum theory rather than relativity theory and the Newtonian classical physics Einstein was committed to. Duration was begging for a more philosophical science able to address metaphysical properties of matter being unfolded in relation with time and space (see Canales, 2015, Chapter 19).[9]

Attunement between organisms, or between organisms and atmospheres, are in fact an echo of a smaller scale. Barad (2007) uses the term "entanglement" to talk about such relationality and the particular qualities it achieves when it is addressed at the quantum level. Barad explains, diffraction – as a property of entanglements – can be taken as a useful counterpoint to reflection: "[B]oth are optical phenomena, but whereas the metaphor of reflection reflects the themes of mirroring and sameness, diffraction is marked by patterns of difference" (2007, 71). In this sense, the distinction between reflection and diffraction works as a correlate in the quantum scale of the distinction between attunement and imitation in the organic scale. Both of them signal the possibility of cross-modal transformation. Diffraction, Barad explains,

> is not a singular event that happens in space and time; rather, it is a dynamism that is integral to spacetimemattering. Diffractions are untimely. Time is out of joint; it is diffracted, broken apart in different directions, noncontemporaneous with itself. Each moment is an infinite multiplicity. 'Now' is not an infinitesimal slice but an infinitely rich condensed node in a changing field diffracted across spacetime in its ongoing iterative repatterning.
>
> (Barad 2014, 169)[10]

Diffraction, like duration, is also about the present – a present whose temporality is complex and goes beyond itself because it contains other events and relations. Diffraction unfolds properties of the present entanglement among space, time, and matter that may convey events and properties from different entanglements and different events but that are being diffracted in this present for example, the possibility of duration bringing in other spacetimes, like "the blowing breeze of the Californian summer" suddenly appearing in the cold winter of New York. This is the richness of diffraction; it helps us notice other temporalities and relations contained in the matter, our wine, and being unfolded by the present event.

The idea of diffraction is about matter's behavior or, better, about matter's dynamic and vibrational nature. Barad, like Bergson, is clear in this quality of matter. For her "matter in its iterative materialization is a dynamic play of in/ stabilities. Matter is never a settled matter. It is always radically open" (Barad, 2012, 214). Material openness in the quantum level is what creates possibilities in the flux of contact and of affection among all kind of qualities, not just in the present duration but in all other possible times and places. "Materiality 'itself' is always already touched by and touching infinite configurations of possible others, other beings and times" (Barad, 2012, 215). In a manner of speaking, matter contains everything that has touched it, and then it allows diffraction of multi-temporal and multi-spacial qualities or what we could feel as feeling connected or being attuned with somebody else. Being part of each other's experience in an intimate way, diffracting time and matter, brings us to the same other place "where we have never been together until now" – that other spacetime that is ourselves and our encounter. This red wine, for example, diffracts rhythms of our bodies into each other in such a promiscuous way that we can touch each other. After a couple of sips, we have been inside each other. But it is by virtue of the diffraction of other relations appearing in the event that we perceive ourselves as moving along such an event; we move from "another space, another time" – to "another us". Such phenomena of diffraction do not belong to the empirical world. As we have seen and as will be further explained in the next section, aesthetic writing focused on aesthetic objects such as wine helps us speculate about them and enrich our analysis.

Stern understood the depth at stake in the attunement; he may have been even imagining diffraction when he asserted, "What is at stake here is nothing less than the shape of and extent of the sharable inner universe" (Stern, 2000, 152). Attunements and diffractions emerge as the continuum of multiple events of cross-modal/cross-scalar transmission of qualities among material bodies. Any of these interchanges are transmissions of qualities and properties. In the transmission, the agent at stake communicates a state in which it has previously been touched or affected (quality), but it also propagates the possibilities of action (properties). This is to say that transmissions are chiefly transmission of affect (Brennan, 2004). Rhythm and vibration are always about affect and the interchanges among bodies that occur "before their translation into actually perceived effects, or the individuated experiences of the relational recomposed entities" (Henriques et al., 2014, 20). Matter is in constant transformation because it has movement as its immanent property; this movement is the vibration that generates patterns of activity that we refer to here as rhythm. Each lapse of a small event in the attunement unfolds and contains temporalities that were not present before but that now can be (cross-modally) expressed. This possibility of presence in the absence is the diffraction. And diffraction is useful to account for aesthetic experience when substantial matter mediates it, especially if we are interested in the sensation of past time or perception. Wine produces its own space-timemattering entanglement. Matter "times". Time matters.

Stern's attunement and Barad's diffraction are of great help here to understand how organic and quantum scales bring to the event some of the multiple durations that Bergson referred to. Bergsonian duration is a philosophically complex concept that is not easy to be translated and used in social sciences committed with an empirical analysis of the observable world. However, affect studies provide us with some of the most sophisticated contributions encouraging us to make a try. As promised at the beginning, this second moment tells you what our substance is made of so you can feel it: a Bergsonian approach to time based on material events, including organic and quantum events, using concepts like attunement and diffraction. This is our texture, our flavor; this is how we taste, what we propose.

Now breathe in. Swallow. Take your time. We are about to keep moving.

Aftertaste: time for perception

Breathe out. When we breathe out the body goes through a state in between relief and awareness; the body gets ready to propose the new pattern of activity, the new rhythm of breathing. Breathing out also intensifies the presence of the aftertaste when we are drinking wine, especially after we swallow. We get the last data, and then we can have a rounder idea about the wine. With all of this information it may sound like we are ready to think about it, to construct our own version of that piece of the world. After swallowing we are ready to represent, to perceive. That is what we are doing in this last moment of the chapter – some final notes of flavor to round out the idea.

There is a fundamental limitation if we understand perception in terms of cognitive production or representation of any kind; we may miss the "presentation", which is of material order while looking for the "re-presentation" within the cognitive domain. Brown and Stenner explain how perception in psychology is commonly understood as mediated by a mental representation of an object; most accounts, they argue, would suggest that "stimuli are perceived by the body, resulting in sensation. This sensation is fed through to the brain where it is converted into mental images (i.e. cognitive representations). These images are then processed in such a way that likely responses can be put into action, if required" (2009, 139, their parenthesis). Brown and Stenner argue that these perspectives attribute a representational function to the brain that "sees perception as a process of elaboration. Sensation is transformed into mental image which is then layered with subjective elements" (2009, 139). Unlike these approaches in psychology, Bergson argued that perception does not elaborate something new that is then added to the existing world. Perception does not construct anything; it subtracts, filters, and reduces certain aspects of the reality. A Bergsonian understanding of perception would be interested in how "we selectively focus upon one aspect of what is already there, which affords certain possibilities for our engagement" (Brown and Stenner, 2009, 140). Such an affordance for engagement suggests a precognitive, material plane of interaction in which the body is already responding; it has been through its own process, and it is already acting upon the objects, affecting and being affected.[11] Thus, as Shaviro (2014b, 2016) suggests, we need of a theory of "discognition".

Representing the wine is not a matter of the present, unlike duration. Representation comes later, with the recursive socialization of the practice around wine, for example, wine training, as Hennion (2007) has proposed. After conscious reflection, we can train our nose; we can "learn to be affected" as Latour (2004) would have it, but it takes more time. In the very event of sharing a glass of wine, all we have is our bodies and our wine. We are here in the timing of the event whose immanent materiality is still to be taken seriously in the study of perception. Bergson was well aware that understanding time in terms of duration is crucial for explaining the material basis of perception. For him, duration is the frame in which "consciousness would grasp, in a single, instantaneous perception, multiple events lying at different points in space; simultaneity would be precisely the possibility of two or more events entering within a single, instantaneous perception" (Bergson, 1965, 45). Duration and simultaneity then, point to the fact that for time to be felt and perceived, there must be always and irremediably a preceding entanglement of spacetimematter. The entanglement is the relational dynamic within which these "multiple events lying at different points" can be perceived together. For Bergson even when "we exist in a 'fluid continuity of the real', we are nevertheless able to actively 'cut out' or 'isolate' discrete forms within that flux" (Brown and Stenner, 2009, 140). Thus, perception provides nothing but provisional "snapshots" within a durational time that always is different from itself. In this captured temporal duration, "affection is not the primary matter of which perception is made; it is rather the impurity with which perception is alloyed" (Bergson, 2005, 58). A Bergsonian understanding of perception then should ask, what aspects of matter or material relations are being subtracted by the process of perception? Our analysis in the "Mouthfeel" section, the second moment, has suggested a way to further explore some of these elements in the experience of sharing wine. In this third moment, we include a couple of notes on the relevance of this perspective to further imagine why it should return to contribute to the study of perception from affect studies.

In the organic and conscious scale, it may seem that time takes its shape by adding one moment after another, then time passes – so does the wine we are drinking – but as Bergson argued, "It is we who are passing when we say time passes; it is the motion before our eyes which, moment by moment, actualizes a complete history given virtually" (Bergson, 1965, 61). Such a motion is mapping the body in relation with the other elements of the entanglement; when Bergson says that "it is we who are passing", he is inviting a shift in the "point of reference" that we are using to account time and perception (which was one of the main conflicts in the debate with Einstein). We can even take the wine as the reference point and try to tell the story from the wine's point of view, in which case we would also be one of the things passing through the elements of the entanglement. As in our wine's time, "Perhaps it is the wine that happens. Perhaps we happen to the wine". As Morton[12] sees it, "This means that when an object is 'translating' another one – when it is influencing it in a causal way – it is doing to that object something analogous to what I as a human do when I act on things" (Morton, 2012, 207). It is as if wine could perceive us.

Regardless of what the point of reference is, when we drink wine a new temporality emerges. Time is an aesthetic property of objects, Morton (2012) would say. These objects are the condition of possibility for quantum diffraction of time, space, and matter that are apparently absent but that can be diffracted by means of the patterns of activity of the matter. And then, once diffracted, these spacetimematterings can be transmitted across scales, a cross-scalar transmission. Perception, then, would be the exercise of the body filtering the entanglement of spacetimemattering of which this body – as matter – is already part. In Bergsonian terms, it is the aggregate of an image;[13] perception is different from matter, Bergson would say, just in degree, not in kind. Perception – and subjectivity in general – is embedded in a material and spatiotemporal process aesthetically expressed that cannot simply be neglected.

Perception for Bergson is about material "willness" for action and movement passing by the human body. "The body, by the place which at each moment it occupies in the universe, indicates the parts and the aspects of matter on which we can lay hold: our perception, which exactly measures our virtual action on things, this limits itself to the objects which actually influence our organs and prepare our movements" (Bergson, 2005, 179). As we argued in the "mouthfeel" matter, vibration is susceptible to be empirically analyzed if we look at its cross-modal and if we speculate about its cross-scalar transmission of patterns. Then as Bergson suspected, "the states of matter can be deduced one from the other"; however, such a deduction is only possible if we "discover, beneath the apparent heterogeneity of sensible qualities, homogeneous elements which lend themselves to calculation" (Bergson, 2005, 204). Organic attunement temporally works to capture a "snapshot" of the past of these homogeneous elements. We can observe the bodies interacting and being part of each other's experience; then the aesthetics of the moment starts appearing. But to bring to experience the registers of material vibrations that are not empirically registrable is not easy. The homogeneity is difficult to be deduced in the smallest scales; due to the rhythmical and vibrational immanence, as Henriques and his colleagues argue, "rhythm as vibration is therefore a force of more-than in that it resolves the apparent finality of matter into molecular becomings. It circumvents the division of reality into bounded beings, and escapes perception even if its movements inform what is sensorily perceived as substances, patterns, and qualities" (Henriques et al., 2014, 19). However, an analysis like ours allows getting the attunements via observation of the interaction between bodies and diffraction via the intuitive description of the aesthetics of the moment through the aesthetic writing. In doing so, we are close to the methodological practice proposed by Anderson and Ash (2015) as a combination of description and speculation.

Attunement "permit(s) one human to 'be with' another in the sense of sharing likely inner experiences on an almost continuous basis. This is exactly our experience of feeling-connectedness, of being in attunement with another. It feels like an unbroken line" (Stern, 2000, 157). Feeling connected is such an important feature of the sensation of the passing of time, but when time passes, certain unconnected things are passing too. Diffraction allows the emergence of such discontinuity (Barad, 2007); it diversifies the present, bringing other entanglements along with their own spacetimematter qualities. Diffraction is also part of the conscious experience, especially when it comes to time: dreams, déjà vu, preemptive memories, hallucinations, fantasies, and imagination – all them share the conscious presence of an absence, a diffraction in the mind.

If all the agents at stake in the entanglement are changing properties and the expression of such changes happens in different registers, there is apparently no reason to keep theorizing perception by thinking that it constructs a version of the world. Rather, if the subjectification of the entanglement is to be useful, it is through the expression of the aesthetics of the experience, which conveys the potential to account for the relations and the affect. Diffractions and attunements may also help because they allow us to focus on the aesthetics of the experience in relation to the timing of the encounter of the bodies (respectively, the organic and the molecular ones). As Morton sees it, "What is called spacetime is the difference between an object's essence and its appearance" (2012, 214). Perception should go there.

The perception of time brings us to the complexities of spacetimemattering. It is therefore important to acknowledge that aesthetic objects produce their own temporal duration; they work as a gravitational center for the aesthetic properties emerging along all the relations in the event. If so, accounting perception and time necessarily begs for an approach to the aesthetic dimension of the materiality of the event. On exploring aesthetics, the potential of aesthetic writing is crucial, as we have advanced in the "Mouthfeel" moment. Barad suggests that "different narrative registers" represent a useful "mode of expressions, not in order to move away from thinking rigorously but, on the contrary, to lure us toward the possibilities of engaging the force of imagination in its materiality. The force of imagination puts us in touch with the possibilities for sensing the insensible, the indeterminate" (Barad, 2012, 216).

We don't write poetry, aesthetic narrations, or experimental writings because we are cheesy or because it is a cool ornamental complement for theory. It is rather a powerful theoretical resource. Poetry is astonishingly important "not because poetry gives meaning to a meaningless mechanism, or because it's the last and best resistance to the juggernaut of modernity, but because poetry tampers directly with causality" (Morton, 2012, 216). Poetry brings to the analysis relations that originally don't dwell in the empirical scale of reality, that is, what Clough (2008) calls the infra-empirical, where she situates affect. Then the resource of an aesthetic writing is important for theoretical reasons; after all, spacetimemattering is about forms and translations, and so is poetry. Particularly in the case of theorizing the passing of time, the aesthetics of the experience, its form, must be close to its account. Our wine's time note, and the whole idea of writing a chapter that "works as a wine tasting" (including the soundtrack for its pairing) is an attempt to bring aesthetic elements to help us understand time and affect. In the case of this chapter, experimental writing is the resource that allows us to speculate about the quantum scale, and the diffractions coming from there, and then to theorize the cross-scalar relation with the organic scale. Aesthetic writing creates new images and new forms; new images help imagination; new forms create new temporalities. This is how we imagine an affective approach to the study of perception, one that brings together organic/conscious and nonconscious and even nonhuman material events emerging through the aesthetics of relations.

By virtue of this speculative aftertaste, an image is being diffracted in our minds: Just imagine: time happening again, Bergson and Einstein getting together over a glass of red wine –the same Californian zinfandel we fell in love with. What possibilities would the material patterns of activity of the substance have brought to this encounter? What kind of diffractions and attunements would have been at stake here, and then how would that have changed the conscious activity, the perception of the world, and the production of knowledge about time? How would an aesthetic object such as a bottle of wine have changed time itself, its history, its future? How would the relation between science and philosophy be perturbed after a bottle of wine? We dreamed such a scene one night while this chapter was being written. Among other things, what the image from our dream makes us suggest is the simple idea that knowledge has more possibilities when it emerges from an entanglement of science, philosophy, and aesthetics. And this is precisely the place for social sciences, at least under the light of affect studies.

Now you have had everything this chapter has. If you like, you can always start the cycle again; like with the wine, you will see how time has changed the way it matters.

Notes

1 Today, the consumption of wine, particularly red wine, is so widespread, and its production so diversified, that the practice of drinking wine is no longer necessarily a luxury commodity (Standage, 2006). Indeed, for it to be a bourgeois practice is rather an exception when compared to the wide range of events, types, and costs now associated with wine. In the same way, knowledge surrounding wine is not – was never – the exclusive property of the upper classes. In fact, the majority of wine produced in the world is by and for the working class. The particular understanding of red wine contained in this chapter comes from two such sources: the little knowledge acquired by the author during more than ten years working as a waiter, and a fifteen-dollar bottle of Californian zinfandel. I write this note, albeit reluctantly, to preempt any cultural – if not classist – assumptions about what it means to share a glass of "wine".

2 This chapter is about the rhythm of an event emerging from unlimited encounters among different kinds of bodies: organisms and molecules mostly. To enact the sensation of rhythm we have chosen red wine as our aesthetic object and organized the chapter into three moments in the experience of tasting wine ("Perspective", "Mouthfeel", "Aftertaste"). In addition, we have decided to pair the chapter with another object whose rhythmical patterns allow resonance and then accompany the sensation evoked. The soundtrack of this chapter is "Three Four" by Third World Love, featuring Israley bass player Omer Avital and jazz

trumpet player Avishai Cohen, and is rhythmically organized in patterns of beats of 3/4 and 6/8 – in other words, in threes.

3 Henri Bergson always wrote in first person plural; this chapter is also written in such form as a small tribute to his philosophy and his writing.

4 The book was originally written in French and published in 1922 under the title of *Durée et Simultanéité*. It was in press at the moment of the debate.

5 See, for example, different arguments about the supposed "missing half second" creating a gap between neural activity and conscious awareness in Massumi (2002), Wetherell (2012), Hansen (2014), Gatens (2014), and Clough (2014).

6 To see common points between Whitehead and Bergson, see Bergson's *Duration and Simultaneity* (1965), especially Chapter 3 about "the nature of time" as well as Whitehead's *Concept of Nature* (1919), especially Chapter 3 on "time". In these passages they explicitly agree and cite each other.

7 Initially known as "Langevin's paradox" and later baptized the "twin paradox", this is explained by Canales in the following way: "According to the Theory of Relativity, two twins, one who traveled outside the earth at a speed close to that of the speed of light and the other one who remained on earth, would meet each other and notice that time had elapsed differently for each of them. Their clocks and calendars would show disagreeing times and dates. The twin who had stayed on earth would have aged more rapidly; time would have slowed down for the one who had traveled. In his controversial book, Bergson denied this to be the case" (2005, 1171). Canales further explains how Bergson's denial of the difference in the clocks brought him many critics and the fame of being the one who does not understand relativity theory.

8 Stern was trying to explore the pre-symbolic communication between infants and their mothers. His point was that the first stage of communication happens by means of an affective attunement between the two bodies.

9 In fact, Einstein was never in agreement with quantum theory as proposed by Bohr; their debate in this sense was another pivotal moment in the history of science. As Barad (2010) explains, Einstein was committed to holding onto a classical ontology, whereas Canales (2015) puts it: Reality cannot be understood simultaneously as a particle and as a wave; they could be one or another but not both at the same time. (For a review on the consistency between Bergson's philosophy of duration and quantum physics, see Canales, 2015, especially Chapter 19.)

10 This quote comes from *Diffracting Diffraction: Cutting Together-Apart* published in 2014. But Barad uses this quote to quote herself in a potential diffracted future. She calls to a footnote that explains "Karen Barad, forthcoming! The reference here is to this very chapter. This may seem a bit strange, and the temporality will already be different once you read this, but it is a gesture to include what is also coming from the future." Let our quote and this footnote be the expression of a spaciotemporal diffraction of Barad's work.

11 We can't generalize and say that all psychologies work with cognitive representations or any kind of representations for that matter (e.g., discursive). Psychology as a discipline is broad, and we could think of proposals like Stenner's (2008) Whitehedian approach to subjectivity; Blackman's (2010) study of modalities of listening and attention, such as voice-hearing that calls for a decoupling of memory, perception, the senses, and the psyche to look for an analytic able to address the intercorporeal transmissions; or even Henriques et al.'s (1984) changing the

subject as an alternative fed by psychodynamic, developmental, and poststructuralist approaches to subjectivity.

12 It may seem counterintuitive to cite Morton in a Bergsonian chapter when he is not a proponent of process philosophies; we believe he would agree with the fact that objects make time, aka the Bergsonian argument that matter is a fundamental vector for time. Morton's arguments about process philosophies privileging the process over the objects is developed in his "OOO defense of poetry" Morton (2012). For a different contrast between OOO and process philosophies, see Shaviro's (2014a) *The Universe of Things*, especially the first chapter, in which Shaviro explains the different disagreements between Harman's and Whitehead's philosophies.

13 Elizabeth Grosz has explained well what "image" means to Bergson: "He defines matter, not in terms of substance or extension, as it has been generally understood in the Cartesian tradition, but in terms of images: matter is the ongoing production or profusion of images. The structure of matter is imaginistic, which is not to claim that it is reduced to the imaginistic perception of a subject (i.e. idealism) or that the image is necessarily or in any privileged manner visual. Matter is conceptualized as midway between the image, so central to idealism, and the object-in-itself, so central to materialism. Matter is an aggregate of images that occasion, in the presence of a perceiver, a series of multisensory perceptions, images capable of representation by many if not all of the senses and by other perceivers" (Grosz, 2004, 163–164).

5 Mezcal and knowledge

In this chapter I will fully develop the last element of our model, the prosthetic object. As explained in the introduction, the prosthetic object expands the capacities of bodies as well as it reproduces bodies' experiences within other bodies, human and nonhuman. To further explain this prosthetic gesture and its relevance to understand human practices embedded in our multilayered model, I will rely on another drinking practice, mezcal drinking, and the correspondent process/object to be looked at within this practice, knowledge. But all of this starts with an anecdote:

In the middle of the summer of 2015, I got a Whatsapp audio. My body shuddered to hear the unmistakable sexiest voice of Mexico City: my beloved Jessica Assai, who happened to be in company of Omar Perez, aka "el Téllez", who would become my mezcal mate and crucial piece for this chapter. I was looking through the window at my apartment in Brooklyn while listening to their proposal: "*Hola, oye*, wouldn't you write some short poetry for the label of a bottle of mezcal?" Something inside shivered. "It is for a special edition for 'Tay Ñuu', el Téllez's mezcal Brand. He is pimping up the brand!" Jessica insisted, throwing small phrases and small silences between them. "The idea is to put short mezcal-related poems in the back labels of the bottles, . . . What do you think? . . . Don't you want your poetry on a bottle? . . . Or what?" I listened, quiet. Then, Téllez picked up the phone and recorded a message himself. "*Qué onda carnal*! Yeah, the idea is to gather poems by different authors and put them on the labels." He continued explaining about his brand and the varieties of mezcal he works with.

We'll get back to the anecdote and the mezcal-poetry project in a minute. But for those of you who still don't know what mezcal is, let me explain first. Mezcal is a spirit distilled from a Mexican endemic plant called "agave". Agave is a scientific name, but Aztecs knew the plant as "metl" or "mexcametl", which later on became the Spanish word "*maguey*". The word "mescal" emerges out of the combination of two Nahuatl roots: "*metl*", meaning agave, and "*ixcalli*", meaning cooked or baked, forming the word "*metzcalt*" or "*metzcalli*" (depending the zone) and eventually getting Spanished up as "mescal". Although mezcal jumped to international recognition in the late 1940s by Malcom Lowry's novel *Under the Volcano* (1947),[1] her cousin tequila is still a little better known, except tequila comes from "agave azul", one specific variety of agave from the at least 150 existent varieties in Mexico. From the rest of the varieties, you obtain mezcal.[2] Recently described by Greene (2017) as an otherworldly drink, mezcal has a complicated history. Bowen (2015) has described how the history of mezcal has been a history of the margins and clandestine nature of production, but it was in 1994 that the National Chamber of Commerce for Mezcal submitted an official petition to register mezcal as a DO (origin denomination) as well as so-called quality standards for mezcal production. There are two enormous problems with these regulations. The first regards the "quality standards", which established a set of norms about how mezcal must be made. Such norms work in favor of industrial production of mezcal at large scale and based on efficiency, whereas they completely ignore the needs and ways of the small producers or the biological variety of mezcal (Bautista et al., 2015). Among the modern technologies there is the "diffuser", used to maximize sugar extraction, and the "distillation column", which is technology used to sacrifice the flavor and complexity of mezcal in favor of less energy consumption and more velocity on distilling. These technologies are meant to speed up production and aim for a mezcal with always the same flavor, which is antithetical to the indigenous systems of productions for which the priority is the dialogue with the plant to understand what is needed to bring out a unique flavor. Traditionally, mezcal production is to create a one-time miracle, not the same one in every bottle produced on a large scale.

The second key problem has to do with the DO. In 1994, only five states were authorized to legally produce mezcal, although more have been included since then but not enough to legitimate all the places that distillate agave. In addition to this, only five varieties of agave were included in that regulation out of forty-five that could and are used to produce mezcal around Mexico. Thus, the real mezcal, handcrafted by a "*maestro mezcalero*" and produced by ancient and indigenous techniques, became illegal in Mexico and in danger of disappearing. This is not a minor detail, the industrialization of mezcal means way more than the systematic precarization of indigenous producers. As if this weren't bad enough, in the long term it means the destruction of mezcal itself as a drinkable cultural expression condensing indigenous knowledge and local forms of living. Greene makes this point by explaining that

> [m]aestros mezcalero are liquid poets, handcrafting their small batches with highly individualized techniques, using plants they have often lived among for years, sometimes decades. Much like skilled French *parfumiers*, maestros mezcaleros are adept at reducing botanical ingredients to particular notes, which, similar to vocabulary in a language, add up to spirits with flavors developed over time by community consensus. In this sense, they are master storytellers – their poetic concoctions the drinkable folklore of their cultures, and the transcendent articulation of dreams.
>
> (Greene, 2017, 96)

Thus, nowadays the mezcal produced by indigenous people using traditional methods needs to apply for the legal status or certification. In some cases it can be done, and in others they can't be certified. Bowen explains:

> There are thousands of mezcaleros who . . . are unwilling or unable to join the formal market for mezcal. Some are outside the boundaries of the DO for mezcal. Others are within the designated territory but do not want to get certified, because it would require them to alter their production practices, or the costs are too high, or they do not trust the regulatory organizations.
>
> (2015, 126)

Then, despite the ancient knowledge artfully materializing in a drinkable piece of culture and history, this is the current context of mezcal in México.

To return to the opening anecdote, el Téllez is a young guy from Oaxaca, which is the spiritual center of mezcal in south México. He is a student that brings real mezcal from Oaxaca (mostly from a region called Sola de Vega) to Mexico City, where he lives. He sells the mezcal so he can pay the bills and survive. He is also the founder of his own small brand called Tay Ñuu, which in Mixtec means "free people". The name is not random. el Téllez militates at an anarchist collective and is part of an anarchist movement of resistance against the norms of standardization of production of mezcal. He believes, and he is right, that standardization in the production of mezcal kills the personal touch of each *maestro mezcalero*. In short, as Téllez explained to me, standardization bastardizes one of the most sacred things we have in Oaxaca: mezcal.

The relationship between mezcal and knowledge is a deep and old one; respectful knowledge is needed to produce, sell, and even drink mezcal properly, so you can really feel it. El Téllez is well aware of this, and the politics of his brand Tay Ñuu take seriously the mezcal-knowledge relationship. He delivers the bottles personally and takes his time to explain to the costumer a couple of things about the variety of agave they are buying, the *maestro mezcalero* that produced it, and the land it comes from. He is concerned in actively enhancing the respect and knowledge his customers have about mezcal, in part, he says, because if they know better, they will enjoy it more. An important feature of the bottles of Tay Ñuu is that they contain the phrase "Orgánico y en Resistencia", meaning organic and resisting (see Figure 5.1). This is an important

Figure 5.1 Front label of Cuixe Tay Ñuu, Orgánico y en Resistencia

political statement. According to Tellez, it is organic because it's made with wild maguey produced without any agrochemicals, and the distillation is done by traditional techniques, which means using Crock-Pots or copper stills. Organic and resisting come together because producing organically necessarily means resisting the legal standardization of production of mezcal previously described.

When Tellez made his poetry proposal, I, of course, said yes. The deadline was short, as they always are, and as any apprentice of scholarship, I had many things to do. So I created a method to hurry up inspiration that I will explain and show within this chapter. I thought that inspiration could not fully arrive at any moment I decided, so I needed to borrow and co-construct inspiration with some help. It was also clear that plants are complex creatures, and I needed to share the experience of getting in touch with the plants to start making sense of them. I designed a method that I call "mezcal encounters".[3] These are events during which I would gather with someone, we would drink one specific variety of agave, the plant mezcal comes from, and we would talk about what we were feeling, trying to pay attention to what the plant did within our bodies. I would make notes describing the shared experience as well as some phrases mentioned during the encounter and write a poem afterward based on the notes. The idea was to get to the core gesture of what that specific agave expresses when it gets in touch with human bodies, or what OOO would call its sensual qualities. So many insights, sensations, and poetry overwhelmed this process that we ended up writing the poems for all the varieties of mezcal Tay Ñuu. Seven poems were conferred to me with the help of seven mezcal mates. The pairing humans and plants were as follows: Jessica and Tobalá, Kuriko and Tepextate, Lorena and Coyote, Angélica and Arroqueño, Thseen and Jabalí, Iris and Cuixe, and Ozuany and Sierra Negra. Mezcal encounters were a method aimed to extract the soul of the plant and turning it into a poem, nothing less. There will be more on this method in a minute.

As I will explain in this chapter, the mezcal encounters worked not only to finish the poetry and create incredible connections with the people and the plants who helped me, but they triggered a thinking process, a knowing process. Like a dog that chases its own tail, I started thinking about thinking, and trying to know about knowing, but beyond the reflexivity and epistemology, the mezcal adventure took me to explore ways to extract the history contained in the plant, to think about the knowledge of agave and what it means for human knowledge to acknowledge the knowledge of a plant (or any nonhuman for that matter). In this chapter, I will share some insights developed during this mezcal and poetry adventure. Three main insights jumped into my head along this process: 1) the epistemological problem of theorizing nonhuman knowledge, plant's knowledge in particular; 2) the potential of poetry as a prosthetic object to speculate about the extension of the plant's knowledge toward human bodies; and 3) the potential of prosthetic objects to connect our three scales of the reality – molecular, organic, and cultural – as well as to work as a function of aesthetic and haptic objects.

Knowledge is sentience is readiness for action, or the plant and the thinker

Mezcal producers that use ancient techniques talk about "knowing the plant". By that they don't mean what would typically be understood by that phrase – a human producing or acquiring knowledge about a plant – they rather mean getting to know, through the senses, what the plant knows, but this way of knowing results in at the least tricky academic discourse. What does it mean that the plant knows something? What kind of knowledge is this? How has it acquired it? And importantly, can we know it? The claim that there is something like a nonhuman knowledge seems pertinent in a time in academia when nonhuman studies are increasing. However the label nonhuman carries a great limitation in its name – the straightforward assumption that there is something human and something that is not so. And one of the problems that comes with such a distinction is that properties associated with humans are hardly thought of as properties of nonhumans. Certainly, if they do something similar to what we do, it's going to be differentiated and will require at least the expansion of the concept. This is precisely what we are going to do here; we are going to expand the notion of knowledge to explain how plants know and how knowledge interchange works through prosthesis to connect different scales of reality.

To understand the problem of nonhuman knowledge, I want to start by proposing a thinking exercise. Let's think about the plant and the thinker. First, say we have a thinker; her name is Kuautontli. She is a trained thinker, a philosopher. Kuautontli knows a great deal; she has been trained within certain philosophical traditions and has developed her own preferences through different schools of thought. Her thinking activity is embedded by and indebted with a historical trajectory made of encounters, some more academic like her encounters with other thinkers, books, tendencies in philosophy, professors during her education, and so on and other encounters more of a personal order, such as lovers, family, friends, the music she listens to, the cities she has studied in, and so on. As a result of this complex trajectory, Kuautontli reproduces certain gestures in her everyday thinking and develops thoughts within specific directions.

Deleuze and Guattari (1994) note that the task of philosophy is the creation of concepts that could be used to think; good concepts then are concepts useful to think about a variety of matters. In a similar spirit, Harman (2016) has claimed that a good philosophy is one that doesn't exclude any entity. Therefore, philosophical thinking appears as the highest expression of the most complex forms of thought – the human one – or so we like to believe. The truth is that in her everyday thinking activity, Kuautontli thinks by releasing a directed flow that has been shaped over the years by her trajectory as a thinker. She is more prone to OOO ideas than process philosophies, but she tries to make it more politically charged because she believes that is important. She cares about neurophilosophy, but she will always prefer Malabou over Edelman; she is a feminist and has decolonial commitments, and so on. And after years of training, she does all this rather automatically. When she thinks, she is not immediately reflecting upon how speculative her thinking is or how politically charged it is. She might do it afterward, of course, as a way of evaluating a thought that has already been produced. We can argue that such an evaluation is necessarily part of the philosopher's task, and therefore part of thinking, but that is not the point. The point is the existence of an activity that is driven by a force that is no longer cognitive, even if it once was. Now it's an organic impulse, a propensity to approach encounters in a certain specific way: a kind of sentience, affect triggering action.

Kuautontli produces thoughts, concepts, and frames of comprehension that can be used to think about different matters, but in addition to being shaped by her trajectory already explained, her thinking exists inside a universe governed by certain rules: she is a reader of philosophy in a public university. This condition is crucial to her thinking, mostly because it pushes the thinking to be expressed in the form of published articles and books; it forces the thoughts to be shared in the format of teaching, or seminars, or conference presentations, and this condition also gives direction to the way she encounters with other thinkers. She has to inform students, to direct their dissertations; she has to debate with other philosophers in international conferences, and so on. In a nutshell, the context that welcomes her thinking also determines the forms, directions, and other expressions of such thoughts. Kuautontli's unintentional flow of thinking is not determined by present cognitive activity, but it is however conditioned in its shape by an arrangement of relations and institutions within which she exists and thinks. Let's leave Kuautontli and her knowledge alone for a minute.

Now, say we got a plant; her name is Metscatli. She is a good plant – a grown one, we can say. Metscatli has been a plant for a long time; she exists in multiple bodies simultaneously. All of them have a given life period, but while some of her bodies die, others are born, so she is always present.[4] Metscatli has also lived a trajectory, equally made of multiple relations of different orders. She has physical relations based on reciprocity, like her relationship with the land that welcomes and houses her bodies and in return gets cleaned by her bodies. In fact, her deal with land makes possible other arrangements, for example, with the mezcal worms, the butterflies, and other neighbor plants like cactus or flowers like the "gualumbo". But all these physical relations are framed by a bigger one: Metscatli's relation with weather and land. Along history Metscatli has decided what weather and land are better for her and her multiple bodies and what environment is better for them to grow strong and beautiful. Along this complex history some of her bodies have decided to live in cliffs so no one bothers them; if you want them you literally have to hunt them. Some other bodies have decided they liked human contact, because some humans take good care of them, and this makes life a little easier. Some like dry weather, some prefer the shadows, some grow as slowly as twenty years, others take only one year, and so on. In short, they have intentionally developed preferences and mechanisms to survive.

In some sense, Metscatli history is not that different from Kuautontli's. Both our plant and our thinker have developed a "know-how" to perform their activities, a practical knowledge that fits pretty much the description of practice we were discussing in the introduction: practice as significant without intending to signify. They both have relationships that move in specific directions, where such a direction is given as a result of historically situated encounters held through years and years of existence. But there is a crucial difference, Kuautontli, our thinker, is human, so she is provided with high cognitive capacities such as language and memory; she is also good at using language (she speaks Nahuatl and English) and reflective thinking. In other words, she knows that she knows; she can rethink what she knows and communicate it efficiently to other humans through language. Metscatl, however, has different resources, such as organic transformative capacities. She changes her colors to let other species know they could come and refresh or even eat some of her leaves and help with cleaning. She also changes her smell to let others (even humans if they know how to smell) know how old she is or to warn other plants about dangers such as plagues. She sends vibrations through the land to remove and inform of the need for different minerals and poses one of the most sophisticated systems of thermoception that along with other senses constitute a particular system of awareness (Chamovitz, 2017). She knows a lot about her surroundings and uses this information to modify her behavior in future encounters, which means she has plant memory (Mancuso, 2018). She is capable of electrical communication among the parts of her body and other plants by using the phloem in her nervous system that is believed to be the key of her sentience (Calvo et al., 2017). The plant processes information even if she is not aware of such processing. This is what Hayles (2017) describes as nonconscious cognition, operations of information processing that occur below the level of awareness. Frost (2016) has also proposed that small organisms, amoeba-like, might have direction without intentions, that is, a knowing how without knowing what and without knowing that they know. Establishing the difference between knowledge and knowledge awareness is important here. We can think about knowledge as a possession of patterns, a propensity that has been imprinted on an organism. A tendency to do things in certain ways, regardless what kind of things we do, could be thinking or changing colors. It's a tendency to express the self in specific forms and interact with other entities in ways that respond to what we know at the moment. Awareness of knowledge requires a different form of subjectivity, the kind that comes with the so-called higher cognitive functions.

As we can see looking at how Mezcatli and Kuautontli exist and relate to the world that surrounds them, there is an important difference in the kind of organoleptic systems that we are equipped with, and not only in the degree in which we can use such systems with awareness. Yet the result seems to share in common one thing: By applying different kinds of information processing we gain awareness of surroundings, and we use that information to redirect different levels of action. Both our plant and our thinker process information to gain awareness about the world and then use such information to redirect behavior, all of this happening with different degrees of awareness of the process. Thus, knowledge prepares organisms to act within given directions. Knowledge provides information about the environment to be aware and then set a course of action. Knowledge is sentience. But not only that, after habits have been developed by repeating the same practice, knowledge becomes the force that predisposes the body to act. Knowledge is readiness for action for both plants and humans. In a similar way that is discussed in Chapter 3 with the chocolate craving, an experience mapped by the body or organism leaves cumulative traces that constitute forces of movement: body knowledge. Thus, knowledge is sentience, is readiness for action.

An understanding of nonhuman knowledge requires the expansion of the idea of knowledge, from a human cognitive-based set of operations toward an organic system of sentience that produces awareness and triggers action. Sentience in humans is filtered by cognition. We think, talk, and classify what we feel; therefore, we take such cognition as the main concern, and we believe it to be what actually creates knowledge about the interactions between bodies and environments. But what stays in the body is actually a mapped sensation resulting from the awareness of relations with the environment. Knowledge is about organic predisposition for action. Indigenous knowledge understood this when dealing with plants in ways to be explained in the next section, but contemporary debates in social theory lack an understanding of knowledge beyond the human. By saying this I don't mean lack of knowledge about the nonhuman. Braidotti (2019), Grusin (2015), and Kohn (2013) are only some examples of the cluster of contributions addressing the nonhuman. What I mean is a lack of understanding of the knowledge that nonhumans possess and use to operate in their environments – not our knowledge of them but their knowledge of whatever they relate to. Nonhuman organisms develop a mechanism of awareness that they use to map experiences and develop a know-how for responses leading to survival. We could dwell, as many biologist and social scientist now do, on the discussion of whether or not "knowledge" is the best word to label what plants do; as interesting as it could be, I have decided to stay with the word "knowledge" to describe a process of passing, communicating, or otherwise replicating trajectories of response to the environment between plants and humans precisely because I find this similarity a productive way to understand nonhuman organisms a little better.

Now, if the knowledge possessed by plant and human involves knowledge awareness for one and environmental awareness for the other, how could they get to know each other, meaning, knowing what the other knows? How can we know what plants know? If their knowing is not full of representations and symbolisms, if it's not codified in a linguistic system, in short, if that knowledge is experienced by plants through a set different organic systems, and there is nothing our knowledge can do to know something that is unknowable, the only resource left is to emulate the plant and try to feel what she feels: to play with temperature, vibrations, colors, smells, and time while feeling the plant to get in touch with her in her own terms. The materialization of the plant experience could be felt, and in doing so we have some access to what the plant was aware of, to what she knew. That is why an experimental method was required.

Of course, this represents a challenge for concepts as old as epistemology. How can we possibly understand a knowledge that is not a human one, that is, a knowledge that is not mediated by linguistic representations, full of reflection and that can be rationally negotiated? What are we going to do with the idea of epistemology after all we have been saying about matter, and nonhuman things, with tendencies and propensities that somehow possess some level of subjectivity, a little bit of intentionality, as Shaviro or Cole would say? If matter does things and knows things, knowledge is no longer a human attribute. Knowledge does not require the highest level of human subjectivity. Knowledge can be known without knowing it just like the simple passing of properties and preferences about where and when to pass it.

If we are able to accept that some knowledge becomes automatic, like speaking your mother tongue or dancing, we accept then that you can know some things without knowing how you know them or without being able to explain to somebody else the mechanisms or logic required to do such activity. You just know it. Even if high cognitive functions were originally involved in the production of that knowledge, they are no longer needed. But even more, in the case of our plant, "decisions" were made without cognitive functions, decisions about where to live, what other organisms are included in the ecosystem, and the rhythm of growing, and so on. Such knowledge has become a way of doing, a habit if you will, a tendency to express yourself and dwell in the world in certain ways, a propensity. It's the same if we talk about our rhythm of breathing or if we talk about someone's tendency to think more like a continental philosopher that as an analytic one. Although Kuautontli surely can explain the difference, she would do so only if asked. In her everyday thinking activity, she is moving by this continental flow in the same way that Mescatli breaths in her surroundings with the know-how developed through centuries by all her bodies. Both breathing and thinking are to some extent plant-like activities; they are tendencies that do not necessarily involve thinking.

But let's talk about how to feel what a plant knows.

Mezcal encounters and the prosthesis of poetics

As mentioned at the beginning of this chapter, mezcal encounters is the name of the method developed to explore knowledge as a process in the relation among humans and plants. The idea was to explore the seven varieties of agave that Tay Ñuu works with, one at the time. Thus, seven encounters were organized: In each of them one variety of agave, a friend, and I would hang out. The friend and I would drink the mezcal, but two important characteristics of the encounters should be mentioned here. First, the mezcal drinking was done using three indigenous techniques meant to send mezcal to different parts of the body and intensify the experience. We drank mezcal the indigenous ways. These techniques produce such an otherworldly experience that the two humans in the encounter start talking, trying to make sense of or share what they are feeling. Thus, the second important characteristic of those encounters was that I would take notes about the experience of the other body as well as my own experience to later compose a poem dedicated to our encounter with that specific plant. As mentioned earlier the poems were then put on the back labels of the bottles and to this day still circulate on the bottles of the brand in Mexico City. I will now explain in detail these two specificities of the encounters, the indigenous techniques, and the prosthetics of poetry.

First, here are the indigenous techniques for mezcal drinking. Three different techniques were used during the mezcal encounters: craving, smoking, and blowing. The three techniques are free adaptations of indigenous techniques. Some of them have been modified from their original versions; however, the whole process of adapting and using these techniques is to play with the fluxes of air entering and exiting the body as well as fluxes of air moving between places inside the body. This is done to modify the physical experience of drinking mezcal, so the people involved in the mezcal encounters felt something that they have never felt, a first encounter, with a substance that most of them have repeatedly tried before. This means that those previous experiences were already mapped in their bodies, already full of meaning, memories, and sense making. Therefore, it was not enough to intensify the experience by conscious means, as in asking the participants to pay attention to what they were feeling. The mezcal encounters were meant to provoke unique experiences by redirecting the encounter between the humans and the plants. The indigenous techniques do this send different qualities of mezcal – smoke, temperature, and smells – to different parts of the human body – pallet, teeth, retronasal smell system, smell nerve in the brain, and so on.

The first technique is called "craving" the mezcal. It is done before tasting the mezcal and has the purpose of preparing the body for the experience, literally creating a body map of the encounter before the encounter happens, and to produce desire for the first sip. It is done by asking the human to close the eyes and moving the cork of the bottle slowly from left to right about five centimeters from their nose, asking them to breathe in intensely when the cork is right under their nostrils – alternating, first right, then left. The eyes are always closed. The human is asked as well to breathe out slowly but firmly, so the next breath in would keep this rhythm. Rhythm is important here; the human has to attune to a stable pattern of breathing. Mezcal smells are so intense that with the help of this craving technique, the bodies are desperate for the first sip.

The second technique is called "smoking". Smoking mezcal has the purpose of quickly sending the mezcal to the brain through the retronasal smell system all the way to the olfactory nerve in the brain. In smoking mezcal, the human body is asked to have a sip from the *jicara*[5] of mezcal, then to move it slowly within the mouth so the whole cavity gets impregnated, and then swallow. Right after swallowing, you strongly suck in air through your mouth with the lips open but teeth close together so the air comes through them. The temperature of the external air creates a contrast with the temperature of the mezcal that then starts warming up. Then the lips close with intense breathing out through the nose. The effect of bringing air in through the mouth and breathing out through the nose, as opposed to breathing in through the nose and breathing out through the mouth, is what sends mezcal molecules to the olfactory system and therefore straight to the brain. The moment of breathing out is extremely intense; most human souls cough and it takes them a little practice to get it. But once you get it, it's a pleasurable sensation of being loose in your own body – by far my favorite.

The last technique is "blowing" the mezcal. Blowing has the purpose of evaporating the mezcal within the mouth, before swallowing, so the multiple notes invade the palate, the lips, and all the nerves within the mouth cavity. Blowing is done by bringing a sip to the mouth but not swallowing, keeping it in the mouth. Move the tongue up and down, letting it hit the mezcal on its way down and triggering mezcal waves within your mouth. The temperature quickly increases, and vapors are realized. After hitting mezcal with the tongue three times, the human is asked to swallow and slowly but firmly blow air through the mouth with the lips almost together and the tongue quiet. Blowing mezcal generally results in a tingling all around the mouth cavity: lips, tongue, palate, gums, inside the cheeks, under the tongue, and other places you wouldn't know you have until you blow mezcal. This technique heightens all the notes in the mezcal, and you feel them from the mouth to the rest of the head.

Craving was used in most of the encounters, but blowing and smoking were sometimes combined, sometimes used in isolation, depending the specific variety of agave that we were working with. Adaptations of other techniques were also used, but here I want to stay with the main three. Generally, the humans were in a state of extreme relaxation, and they would say phrases to describe the physical experience in their bodies after using one of the techniques: "I feel a wind that make me stand up, and I feel someone is behind my head", "I feel the movement of a root becoming three if I breathe; I feel it in my head", "I can hear what happens inside my body, but it's a sound that doesn't sound; it's a movement", and so on. Bodies were changing. clearly experiencing something for the first time. I would make notes of all kind of comments, and as we continued drinking, we would keep describing the experience. In addition to the corporeal experience, there was also a lot of description of environments and atmospheres that seemed to take over the mezcal encounter" "feels like I was in an old place from my childhood, surrounded by burning wood", "I can feel the sky becoming red with my closed eyes", "I feel connected to the ground, like the ground was an extension of my body". Surroundings were changing. Humans were suddenly able to feel the air, temperature, land or even the energy from other spaces. There were also expressions of anthropomorphization of the plant, things like "my palate is now like someone with a big personality just walked in", "an old spirit just made itself present, but it was actually always here". This anthropomorphization sometimes had the form of intentionality, like in "it wants me to say her name", "its life that broke through and now has come to teach me", and so on. All these forms of acknowledgment of the other agency either by referring to the presence, the essence, or the intention shared in common the idea that this presence is strong, takes over, and knows what it's doing; that came across in all seven encounters. Other beings entered the encounter. But for me the most interesting phrases were those describing a blurring line between human and plant. Humans described experiences of feeling like they were something else: "You start thinking in mezcal language, no longer human words", "I feel like old wood writhing, encountering the fire – overwhelming pleasure, like a mountain that knows about time", "It's taking over and makes me be like her, happy to be dry, like a worm that forgets what she knows". I bring these short notes to point to the fact that during the mezcal encounters, humans experienced a modification of the self-awareness systems of their bodies and described sensations that were felt for the first time in their lives. This self-awareness was in relation with the mezcal and their bodies, the experience they felt as individuals, or between their bodies and something else – the air, the light, and so on. This is the experience of others being in touch. But the interesting and most poetic one is of a third kind: the experience of becoming something else. This is an experience of no longer feeling like a human but feeling like something else. Some of the human souls described this as becoming the plant. And it was acknowledged in the seven encounters that the plant knew you were trying to get in contact, sometimes resisting, sometimes trying to help them figure it out, sometimes appreciating and welcoming them, and so on.

I share these notes not as an attempt of analyzing the experience; my intention was always to make poetry of it, not to analyze it. Plus, the analysis of human experience is always limited by human ways of accountability, so there is nothing interesting to explore there if we are to understand and take seriously the nonhuman. In addition to this, it was clear that during our mezcal encounters, the humanness of the participants got compromised. Thus, this nonhuman experience allows me to make a theoretical point of more relevance for our multilayered model. What our indigenous techniques for mezcal drinking were doing was simply to trigger events in the molecular scale that were unknown by the conscious processes in the organic scale. As such events resulted from the liquid plants entering our bodies, OOO would suggest that the interchange of properties between these two objects, mezcal and a body, could only happen by virtue of the sensual properties interacting in an aesthetic plane of causality. But it is right there where something else happened. The aesthetic domain triggered unexpected experiences, the first time in lived experiences in contact with an object that most of them had encountered beforehand. This suggests that it is not only the sensual qualities but the very nature of the encounter that determines if a property is sensual or not; even more, it could be the case that an allegedly real property to which we have no access becomes sensual given a change in the pattern of interaction. The ontology of the object, the plant in this case, precedes the encounter, sure, but it's also modified on it; therefore, it's both previous and precedent to the encounter. This is why it is so important to combine objects and process in the analysis of practices because in analyzing practices like drinking mezcal, it becomes clear that the ontology of entities is stable, and simultaneously it is not.

I'm not suggesting that we access the real object within the plant rather that some of the real qualities might have become sensual qualities and then appeared in the encounter. That is what I think represents an emulation of the plant – the possibility of feeling a quality that we would never experience by rational means in the organic scale. Attention and focusing on the experience wouldn't be enough; a different experience needs to be had for other qualities to appear in the encounter. That is what indigenous knowledge does, plays with the scales and challenges rationality by giving us access to the traces of other entities' experiences; that is how indigenous knowledge is better equipped to understand the nonhuman because, among other things, they have a different approach to the capacities of the human body and a special understanding of how to expand such capacities to escape the human condition. The plant knowledge can't be known; it must be felt. What the indigenous techniques of mezcal drinking allow is to take an object in the organic scale, such as the human consciousness, and take it out of its Western-established forms of existence to use other capacities, untouched for most people.

A poem was written from the notes of each encounter and put on the back label of the corresponding bottle as an effort to capture the wholeness of the encounter with the different plants (see Figures 5.2 and 5.3).

Figure 5.2 Arroqueño, Cuixe, and Jabali Tay Ñuu, back labels featuring the image of the agave

Figure 5.3 Tepextate Tay Ñuu next to jicaras con anillos

I want to move now to explain a couple of things about the prosthetic nature of the poems and the reason they can importantly contribute to the understanding of nonhuman knowledge and therefore the reconfiguration of the very idea of knowledge.

Trying to not fall into what Smith and Morra (2006) recognize as a "metaphorical opportunism" in the use of prosthesis, my use of prosthesis is not a metaphorical one. It refers to an analogous extension of body states reached by means of objects. Of course, there are numerous precedents in the use of the prosthetic notion. In times of post-structuralism, Derrida featured text as mind prosthesis, as a device that reflects conscious thoughts. By the late 1990s, however, Hayles was featuring the body as first prostheses and a matrix for prosthesis when she claimed "the posthuman view thinks of the body as the original prosthesis we all learn to manipulate, so that extending or replacing the body with other prostheses becomes a continuation of a process that began before we were born" (Hayles, 1999, 3). Little after that and based on phenomenology, Hansen (2006) would feature human skin as the originary technicity and therefore the first prosthetic mechanism between the inside and the outside world. But, as explained before, I'm understanding a prosthetic object as an object that increases the capacity of organisms; they expand bodies' experiences in at least two directions, either increasing the input of the sensation triggered by the interchange of sensual qualities or increasing the possibility of expanding the experience of the body beyond itself, increasing the output directed toward other bodies, getting close to a reproduction of the experience in another body. These prosthetic objects work as an extension for the body because they let bodies reach other bodies but also because they allow bodies to feel more and to be reached in different and new ways, like the bodies of the humans in our mezcal encounters.

The first prosthetic gesture, expanding the sensual domain of bodies, leads eventually to expand the perceptual domain. This is relevant because all these new experiences work as a basis for different understandings of the world; it is understanding of the relationships in which another body is embedded. For the bodies' experiences to be expanded, the real qualities of the prosthetic object must withdraw from encounters and let their sensual qualities produce a new perceptual object, a sensation. The second prostatic gesture expands the output and reproduces the experience, working by reaching beyond the original interchange of sensual qualities. The nature of the encounter needs to be modified, as happened in the mezcal encounters, so the capacity for sensorial output can be amplified and new sensual qualities appear in the encounter. This means that the prosthetic object increases the capacity of the sensual qualities in other objects through the expansion of other bodies' experiences, but it also modifies the sensual qualities participating in the encounter. Prosthetic objects might variate in their sensual qualities, but the real qualities are shared with the body it expands, that is, the part of the prosthetic object that can't be felt but makes bodies feel.

Poetry is a great example of prosthetic object. Poetry has the capacity to expand a body's experience toward another body to make it feel the sensual qualities of the encounters in which such a body has partaken. The relevance of prosthetic objects is the way they challenge the logic of the organic scale in which, according to phenomenology, a body can experience only the encounters in which it participates. Well, the virtue of prosthesis is that it breaks this rule. Thus, if the body's number one experience encounters and then develops prosthetic means to a concrete object, some of the qualities of this encounter can be experienced by a second body, even if this second body didn't participate in the encounter or even if the second body has never even imagined such an encounter. Poetry creates images in which relations of causality are at stake, and such images and such relations of causality resonate in a body that reads poetry. According to Morton, "When an object influences another one, it does so by translating that object. The Greek for translation is metaphor" (2012, 206). This sort of translation between objects is the raw material for the human or nonhuman experience that poetry can capture. Morton claims that the theoretical relevance of poetry goes far beyond the meaning of poems; they carry seeds for ontological transformations. "To study a poem is not to study meaning alone, even if we expand 'meaning' beyond established parameters. To study a poem, rather, is to see how causality operates. A poem directly intervenes in reality in a causal way. . . . Poems do something as physical as what happens when my car scrapes the sidewalk" (Morton, 2012, 206).

We can say in a general sense that all language or communication can work as prosthesis in some degree. Derrida argued long ago for the prosthetic qualities of language, as long as language is able to bring bodies into affective dynamics and therefore in the production of sensitivities and meaning, although the intensity of sensual qualities is necessary in poetry and not a requirement in all other forms of language. Poetry is meant to make you feel specific feelings that the author wants you to feel. Even if a great speech or a great conversation can potentially have prosthetic effects, that is not the rule. Colombian poet William Ospina (2003) has claimed that poems are conferred to him, that there are some poems that he would have liked to write but were not conferred to him and other poems that make him wonder how he could possibly write poetry on a topic of complex sensibilities like war or desolation. Beyond the poetic license of this claiming, the autonomy of a poem as an object with an independent life from the author and the objects included in it is what makes a poem prosthetic. It carries the seeds of experiences that could be felt and that don't belong to the author or any of the words or objects mentioned in the poem.

As mentioned in Chapter 4, both poetry and experimental writing are not relevant out of their ornamental qualities. They are relevant for theoretical reasons; they are raw material for speculation, and they are windows to events that couldn't be accessed from our human condition in the organic scale of reality (Figure 5.4).

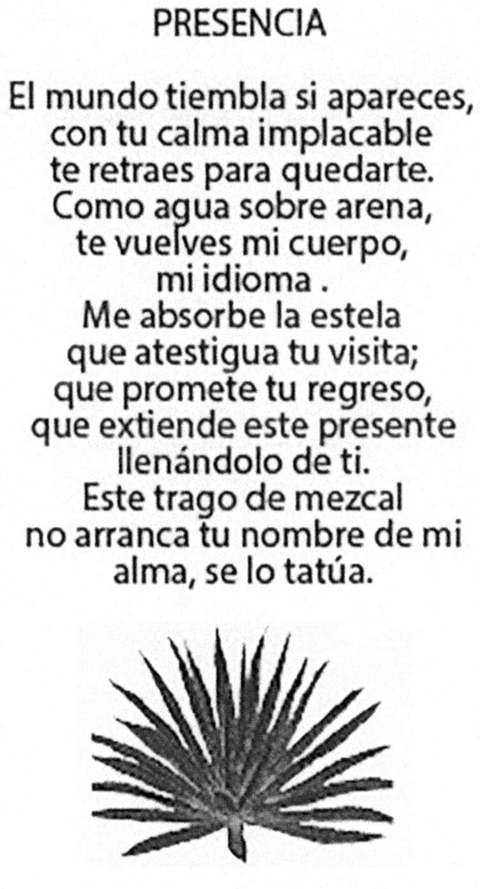

Figure 5.4 Back label of Arroqueño Tay Ñuu, including the image of an agave Arroqueño

Three notes toward nonhuman knowledge

Understanding nonhuman knowledge requires understanding knowledge as sentience and readiness for action. This idea requires a whole *reconfiguration of Western epistemologies* toward an approach more concerned about the complexities of the practice and the ways in which practical knowledge is actually used to mediate relations and less about legitimacy or procedures for the knowledge. This means for epistemology to take seriously nonhuman subjectivity and particularly the capacity of nonhuman agencies to develop a cumulative sensitive experience that then results in tendencies with direction in encounters with other bodies – a "knowing how" that is not mediated by discourse or representation.

A key element for the understanding of the nonhuman is the *prosthetic gestures* of such organisms. Precisely because their practical knowledge is not meaning mediated, what nonhumans use to relate to their environment and other organisms is prosthetic technology that communicates practical and/or transcendental necessities. Prosthetic objects are also good to understand the relations among the three scales of reality and the other aesthetic dimensions as occurred within a practice. This means that prosthetic objects can translate an encounter in the molecular scale into a sensitive or perceptible event within the organic scale, or an encounter in the organic scale – like human-nonhuman encounters – could be translated into something known and shared in the cultural scale (like a poem). But in a similar manner prosthesis can work as a function of haptic or aesthetic objects that explains events connecting the aesthetic dimensions of reality, like a smell that makes you feel plant.

Poems in particular are relevant when the unit of analysis is a human practice, for poems carry cultural implications and develop trends and cultural ways of feeling. They key challenge that prosthetic objects represent for OOO is the idea that objects do not carry predispositions to relate; it is not given what qualities are to withdraw the encounters. Even if both objects have stable sensory systems like plants and humans do, exploring what organisms can do means being able to trigger ontological transformation during the encounters. Ontology is both preceding the encounter and modified by it.

Scales are planes of activity with internal processes that dynamite the inner life of these scales, but objects as defined by Harman can't be reduced to their components or effects; objects have parts that we cannot access because they withdraw the encounter. It is my theory that if we need objects in a cross-scalar–cross-dimensional model, it is because what is not accessible in certain scales might be inherited by activity coming from another scale. Objects connect scales of reality because they carry qualities and components; some of them become sensual, some real, so we need to understand the object as an entity in the middle because our access to objects occurs in different ways in different scales.

Indigenous knowledge has a variety of prosthetic technologies (from drugs to ways of breathing) that are meant to enhance the capacities of human bodies precisely so we can be more aware of experiences lived by others. The practicality of indigenous cosmogonies is an element that hasn't been explored in depth; when we care about indigenous people, as an academic gesture, we care about their knowledge, as in their ways of understanding. Ignoring that, at least in some traditions like the Aztec one, some of their ways of understanding were actually not discourses about frames of comprehension but rather ways of doing and being in the world. Knowing the plant means knowing what the plant needs to grow strong and beautiful and to be able to provide the best spirit. If you know the plant, then you are able to take care of the plant and take its life in that direction. This means that the plant is going to help you produce the mezcal you want because the organism that is the plant, when it is treated that way it develops tendencies and propensities, or what I want to call plant knowledge, an understanding of what you want as a human being, the plant knows what you want and then produces it. If there is a short way of saying this, it would be in knowing the plant, the plant gets to know you and knows what you want from her. Miracles like mezcal are actually possible because of this interchange of knowledge beyond the human.

Knowledge production and transmission involve a life experience that is physical rather than purely symbolic or meaningful. An approach to what nonhumans know has to involve moments of physical transformation to extend our sentience. Knowledge is sentience is readiness for action. Prosthetic objects like poems help us access nonhuman knowledge by reproducing elements of the sentience of the nonhumans at stake. Although some qualities of the nonhuman object will always be withdrawn from the encounter with the human, experimenting with the body to reconfigure the organolepsis opens up the human to new relations. This is what indigenous drinking techniques for mezcal have done for our bodies in this mezcal journey. Producing new corporeal experiences helps us imagine what a plant was aware of, and poetry as a prosthetic object throws the potential for affective capacity in the reader, although it requires to be actualized by deep connections with both the mezcal and the poetry to feel and therefore know.

**In bold, the titles. Under them, in parentheses and italics, is the plant they are dedicated to. Here the poems we wrote:*

Ecos

(Tepextate)

Sólidas y delirantes huellas,
ecos de otros cuerpos en el mío,
tierra en resistencia gota a gota,
ecos sin oídos, ni ojos, ni pena

Un pinchazo en el exhalo,
ecos sobreviven ciertos gestos;
ecos se evaporan y perdonan
la frágil vanidad de cada trago

Ecos que expanden cuerpos,
réplicas de vida y fuego,
ecos que emanan tiempo
en mi corazón de Tepextate.

Caricias

(Coyote)

Un gesto inesperado
que bifurca cicatrices,
una traición que desata
placer incontrolable.
Un dragón que mira,
exhala y vuelve;
un cielo que enrojece,
ríe, y siente
la caricia en que
el coyote supo todo.

Piedra

(Tobalá)

Vida discreta,
implacable
formas hostiles,
ígneas
mágica supervivencia,
placer
vida eterna.

Brisa

(Jabalí)

Vuela una imagen,
como jabalina
rompe el viento
Vuela hacia
un lugar que es mío,
que desconozco
Pasa, abre el tiempo
y el misterio de un cuerpo
en su propia compañía
Sopla el jabalí
todo se pasma.

Presencia

(Arroqueño)

El mundo tiembla si apareces,
con tu calma implacable
te retraes para quedarte,
como agua sobre arena
te vuelves mi cuerpo, mi idioma.

Me absorbe la estela
que atestigua tu visita,
que promete tu regreso,
que extiende este presente
llenándolo de ti.

Este trago de mezcal
no arranca tu nombre
de mi alma, se lo tatúa.

Tierra

(Cuixe)

En esta danza,
perfecta y vieja,
sólo una fuerza
lleva el paso.

Sigilosa, como
sabiéndose dueña,
entra y encuentra
un dolor, quizá
antiguo o inadvertido;
lo cura y sigue
siempre bailando.

Celosa del secreto,
permite sentir,
pero nunca saber
y, sin embargo,
en un suspiro humilde
te entregas siempre
en su regazo.

Sierra abajo

(Sierra Negra)

Chacotea un erizo de miel
en leña vieja,
untado en hojas de otro pueblo;
y hasta los cuencos cantan
celebrando su dulzura
y ríen lágrimas de tu boca
olvidando su dolor, su placer.
Es un movimiento agónico
pero que igual sorprende,
es la novedad decadente,
un viejo bailando en el *afterparty*,
un trago de verdad
y el gesto último de vida.
Es la última primera vez.

Notes

1 Although this novel is known to be nicely written, the book depicts a man who is trying to drink to his dead in Mexico, which hugely contributed to the image of mezcal as addictive and to the Mexican drinking culture as one of excess; both of these things are misconceptions of the actual indigenous practice around drinking. This novel is rather disrespectful to the sacredness around mezcal.

2 There are 200 varieties of agave in total; 150 are endemic of Mexico, only forty-two of which are used to produce mescal.

3 Thanks to Rachel Liebert for helping me come up with this term.

4 In Aztec cosmogony a plant (and most nonhuman entities) have essence that is shared by its multiple bodies. What we call a plant species is the nonhuman entity, and every single plant that belongs to that species is an expression of such nonhuman essence, one of her bodies.

5 Traditionally, you drink mezcal in a "jicara", as Janzen, 2017 explains it, "born out of necessity during the early days of mezcal production, the rugged looking jicara is actually half of a hollowed-out ground. Thanks to its shape and shallow depth, mezcal rests neatly in the bottom while the aromas float freely into the air. Jicaras add a rustic feel to a nip of mezcal, but they do have downsides: they're almost impossible to clean (soap residue often clings to the inside) and they aren't easy to resto on a table due to the curved base" (Janzen, 2017, 121).

6 Toward a multilayered model to digest reality

This last short section has as a twofold purpose: first to summarize the contribution of a multilayered model of reality to the understanding of human subjectivity and how this understanding of human subjectivity is nonhuman-centered as illustrated throughout the chapters. Second, in this section I also want to describe what the politics of *Digesting Reality* are, particularly in relation to the production of knowledge and therefore the combined use of process philosophies and OOO in this book.

Digesting subjectivity

In the previous chapters, I have made an effort to illustrate how the multilayered model can contribute to the understanding of human subjectivity from what I've called a nonhuman-centered study of human affairs. To understand exactly what is new in this approach, we need to understand how subjectivity, and human minds for that matter, have been approached by social theorists in recent years. I'm not going to offer here an exhaustive revision of the main theories – that is a job for another book – rather, I want to mention only a couple of main gestures shared in common among the main approaches to the study of subjectivity during the second half of twentieth century and the beginning of twenty-first century to make clear what *Digesting Reality* is adding to the equation.

The production of subjectivity has been mainly studied as a process of formation of individual or even relatively sharing minds by virtue of a system or assemblage that is articulated around them, which then affects the ways humans understand the world they live in. For example, in the post-structural tradition, the system of assemblage that shapes human minds and ultimately subjectivity has been featured as social agreements or constructions. It's even been agreed that such arrangements are mobilized specifically by language. What shapes human subjectivity has also been understood as well as a social structure within which individuals gain different positions that come with a political mindset, as in ideology theories. In a general sense, the ways in which different social systems shape human minds by influence of institutions, subsystems, ideology, or cognitive capacities like language or memory, and so on have been characterized by the study of the relationship between these systems that somehow act beyond the individual (culture, ideology, institutions, etc.) and the individual minds that are shaped by them. If we explain this theoretical gesture in terms of our multilayered model that we presented in the introduction of this book, it would correspond to the study of the influence of the cultural scale on the human mind dwelling in the organic scale in the case of institutions, ideology, and so on or the study of purely human relations and their representation in the organic scale, like in the case of certain discursive studies or even phenomenology, where whatever the subjects experience is represented with the help of language and the sum of these experiences shapes human minds. In the best case, this is a bidirectional study of the effects of cultural and organic scales.

By the end of the twentieth century, perspectives like ANT or even STS have pointed to the relevance of objects or agencies around us and their important role in the configuration of the social. Although this contribution is important, it does not bring "the social" outside the representation that we, "the theorist", can produce about the ways in which we "human beings" represent the world. It's like a double anthropocentrism. First is how we (scientists) produce knowledge, and then making all this knowledge about how we (humans) understand the world. Anthropocentrism and the consubstantial epistemological focus, or what OOO would call correlationism, has been signature in the ways we have been approaching the human mind. Even when the focus is put in something that is not us, its study necessarily becomes the study of the ways in which we represent it and, therefore, is anthropocentric and epistemologically centered.

By the beginning of twenty-first century, approaches such as affect studies, new materials, and nonhuman studies pointed out the relevance of matter in social life. Importantly, the role of matter, nonhumans, and processes of affect and being affected made it to the center of social theory. As enlightening as this has been, acknowledging agency in material and nonhumans has only meant the agency to do things or affect other objects in their material dimension. Either in relations among nonhuman, like those described by Kohn (2013) in the jungle, or talking about relationships between humans and nonhumans, like Despret's (2004) study on the horse-human relationship, the focus has been on 1) how they (nonhumans) modify each other's capacities to act or 2) how the nonhumans modify our human capacities to feel, do, or act with our bodies. However, throughout the chapters, I have been looking to a third question: how material agencies, either human or not, carry processes and qualities that can shape the way we think and produce understandings of the world around us. This is how material nonhuman forces can shape human subjectivity, not because thinking about them makes us think new thoughts, not by modifying the content of our thinking, but rather the shape and the tendencies and propensities of this thinking to produce new thoughts. My goal here is to show how material, nonhuman, affective processes create a whole new predisposition for subjectivity production. In everyday practices, through material mediation, a new form of subjectivity production is produced.

Translating to our multilayered model (see Figure 6.1), the study human of subjectivity during 20th century is represented by the line "A", a straight, unidirectional link from the cultural scale to the organic one, understanding subjectivity as the process of the human mind's shaping and regulating done by institutions and social systems, social representations, or constructions, and so on. The line "B" represents the first thing I want to add to the equation, an understanding of how material events in the molecular scale of reality affect not only body capacities but the very shapes of our thoughts.

What I offer for a nonhuman-centered approach of human subjectivity is the inclusion of the processes going on inside the molecular scale of activity and a system of speculation between such a molecular activity and the shaping of subjectivity. The way to do it is by considering the

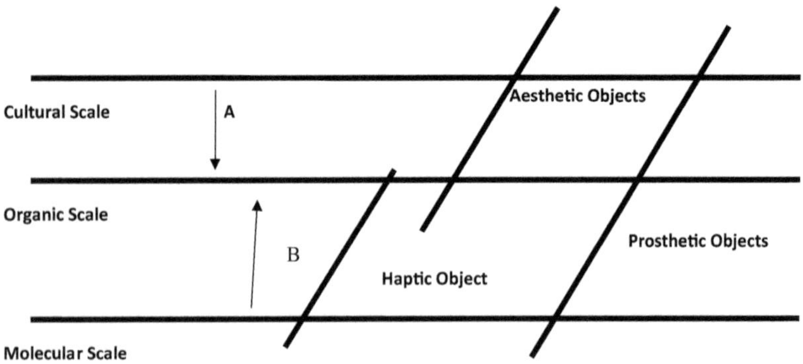

Figure 6.1 Three scales of reality and three aesthetic dimensions

human body as an ontological exceeding the human mind. This means that the body has capacities and processes that bypass human consciousness, ones that are not necessarily registered by it and yet feed forward some tendencies and propensities to the emergence of subjective processes. The reason this book focuses on everyday human practices is because this is the way we approach this exceeding body, by looking at how the practice reconfigures activity in our three scales of the reality, how the aesthetic objects emerging during the practice add to the organic base for the production of subjectivity, and consequently, what kind of subjectivity is welcome or pursued by these kinds of bodies. This system, half description of the material, half speculation of the multilayered effects, is for me the direction that needs to be followed to develop what Harman (2011a) imagined as a speculative psychology. I wouldn't go as far as to say that my proposal brings the basis for an speculative psychology; my goal was rather more humble: All I wanted to do was to decentralize the study of subjectivity to understand the human mind as something that is not individual, is not made of representations, doesn't work with lineal relations of causality, and especially, is open to the nonhuman and all materialities in ways that consciousness can't process and yet can be modified by them. It is not a Cartesian approach. If I say that the human body is an ontological excess of the mind, this does not mean ontologically independent; it means that body includes consciousness but goes beyond it. And if we are to understand how the human mind works, we need to understand the things about the body that we are not aware of, of whose relationships with consciousness hasn't been explored yet.

In addition to including the molecular scale to explain human subjectivity, my approach also includes analysis of our three objects and the ways they shape human subjectivity production. In terms of the multilayered model, the study of subjectivity that I propose includes the study of the reciprocal relations between the cultural and organic scales (arrow A) but also a reciprocal relation between the molecular scale and organic scales (arrow B), the study of the effects of haptic, aesthetic, and prosthetic objects in the subjectivity being produced in the organic scale (arrows C, D, and E), and more importantly the relations among arrows A, B, C, D, and E, which are closer to an ecological understanding of human subjectivity that centers the body but not the human mind (see Figure 6.2).

In Chapter 1, for example, I explored how a drop of sweat, as a haptic object emerging from a molecular process, redirects the attention of individuals in the organic scale and how after the practice of eating street tacos have been ritualized through decades of repetition, the thermal

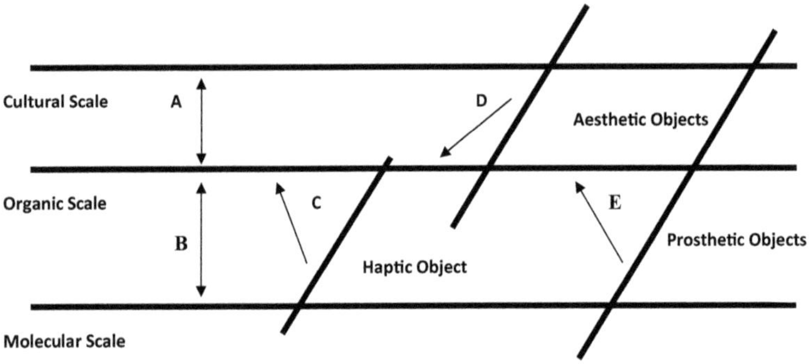

Figure 6.2 This is how social sciences should look like!

components of our eating practice have developed a cultural correlate, the emotion of ansias, to which Mexicans relate in a particular way. This is an example of engaging with some of these arrows, mainly A, B, C, and D. Chapter 2 on the politics of veganism adds the exploration of the haptic and aesthetic objects like smell, skin texture, vegan dishes, and places in creating a body that is predisposed to certain ways of thinking about the politics of food. This is mainly arrows C and D, but this chapter also describes the processes in the three scales of our reality, which would be A and B. The chocolate chapter, for example, explores more the molecular and organic relations (A and B), focusing on the production of desire, looking at how ways of thinking about eating are shaped by material processes that bypass consciousness, like economy, policies, food and regulation, but also mirror neurons and smell processes. The wine chapter also focuses on the relations between the molecular and organic. That was an example of mostly arrows B and C. This is how a multilayered understanding of the way we digest reality helps expand our comprehension of human subjectivity beyond anthropocentrism and correlationism.

The politics of *Digesting Reality*

Digesting Reality is a project whose purpose of course is to help us understand reality better. But in doing that, I have made choices, and such choices have an agenda behind them. First, I have decided to develop a multilayered model to explore human subjectivity from a nonhuman-centred approach and to do it through the analysis of everyday practices like eating and drinking. Second, I have also chosen to develop my model by combining process philosophies with OOO and some contributions from sciences like molecular biology, neuroplasticity, and quantum physics, and I have also used aesthetic elements like poetry and experimental writing. In this last bit of the book, I want to be explicit about the reasons behind my choices: the politics of *Digesting Reality*.

The first choice was motivated by an urgency to move humans away from the epicenter of the production of knowledge. I have acknowledged throughout the book that I'm not the only one with this commitment, and a lot of efforts have been made in such regard. However, the addition of the molecular scale and the typology of my three objects adds something to such efforts: to acknowledge that nonhumans don't belong exclusively to what we can empirically recognize as nonhumans, with our still visually centered idea of the empirical and the technological mediation that is also designed to see small things. Nonhumans are also odors, heats, textures, shapes, and other nonmaterial entities like the presences that entered the mezcal encounters in Chapter 5. This is important, because if we reduce the nonhumans to what we can empirically recognize as nonhumans, then our understanding of the nonhuman is still human centered. This is why a serious nonhuman, decolonial approach can't be an evidence-based approach and therefore can't have epistemological commitments.

This is crucial for the theorization of human subjectivity because despite neuroscience's efforts to make available access to neurons, networks, and bloodstreams in the brain through technological mediation, in everyday life there is a good amount of nonhuman agencies that are not considered. Most of the neglected nonhuman objects are objects that emerge from our bodies, like odors, or objects that create an assemblage and a meta-object that wraps us without us knowing, like an atmosphere, or objects that act on behalf of other bodies and therefore get neglected, like poems. That is the reason I created the typology of haptic, aesthetic, and prosthetic objects to include this aesthetic dimension of life, to name them and include them in a theory of subjectivity. The aesthetic dimension of what I have called the "analogous reality" remains disconnected from subjectivity production, perhaps because human minds are rarely thought of as aesthetic objects that can be affected in their aesthetic dimension. If we think about the mind as an object, it's clear that what is affected in its interactions is only the aesthetic surface, the shape of our thoughts. This aesthetics of the mind is what my proposal brings out of the necessity of further advancing the decentralization of the production of knowledge – bringing the nonhuman beyond human empiricism and toward the aesthetic dimension of life, to develop a less rational, less evidence-based, less epistemologically violent, less ontologically obsessed approach to understand our reality.

The political agenda behind my second choice, to combine process and objects, and science and aesthetic elements to shape my approach, is also to be clarified. It's been largely argued that the philosophical basis for knowledge production in social sciences and social theory require revision. The turn to affect, new materialism, and nonhuman studies is evidence of and a response to such a necessity. So is the philosophical debate within the continental school about process and objects, where the main question is, what is the analytical unit that better accounts for the reality we live in?

With some exceptions, poststructuralism was characterized by an epistemological commitment or at least a desire to create a model for the production of knowledge that was consistent, evidence-based, and rational. This created problems in the second half of the twentieth century that required a response (Lara, 2015). It was there where the philosophical basis of knowledge was rethought and a lot of "turns" took place; affect, new materialism, nonhuman studies, and so on took an ontological commitment as the main gesture of early twenty-first-century social science. However, this came with its own problems, for example, the lack of understanding of human subjectivity and the problematic politics of ontologically centered models (Lara et al., 2017). My point here is that both epistemological and ontological commitments in knowledge production germinate problems for different reasons. The first is essentially anthropocentric; the second is politically problematic and neglects the subject as a subjectivity producer.

In my view, knowledge production must have at the base of all its apparatus a political project, not an epistemological or ontological one. The drive and main criteria at the center of the production of knowledge must be politics.

But why politics? If we consider perspectives that claim to not be interested in politics, like OOO, we can find hugely problematic effects. OOO explicitly rejects political commitments, particularly those associated with leftist ideology, gender politics, race, or any commitment with social justice as we already explained in the introduction of this book. Although I agree with Harman that politics shouldn't be restricted to human affairs, I can't but reject his idea that politics shouldn't be about relations of power and dominance, not for social theory. Chapter 2 makes a clear proposal of how to expand the notion of politics toward the aesthetic dimension of life without excluding the relations of power that we live under and address the complexity of politics in a way that is still relevant to understand social problems and events.

In *A Theory of Everything* Harman makes an analysis of the American Civil War in which he focuses on looking at the "number of points at which the conflict might have been preempted" to identify "when did the Civil War really begin?" (2018, 117). As interesting as this analysis is, there is no trace of how finding out how when the Civil War starts and ends helps prevent or even understand social phenomena like this, let alone any mention of slavery or any other process with current consequences in the real world. This is because Harman is rather interested in avoiding what he calls "the often excessive devotion in social theory to talk of oppression, exploitation and domination" (2018, 113).

Neglecting the social injustice of events is a common gesture for Harman; in *Immaterialism* (2016) he does something similar while analyzing the Dutch East Indian Company. He claims,

> When Western Empires are discussed in our time, exploitation and domination are usually the first thought on everyone's minds, and too often the only thoughts. In what follows, we will encounter cases of injustice and cruelty that no nation should aspire to repeat. Yet we should also not exaggerate European dominance, given the failure of Western powers to make hegemonic inroads in Tokugawa. (37–38)

And then he continues by making a list of places that were not occupied by European forces. He mentions a couple of more injustices made by the company, like the fact that they "forced local people to resettle at locations convenient for its own operations" (39) just to conclude that all this shouldn't be important in the analysis. He suggests that social theories should be concerned with doing ontologies of objects. Harman suggests, "If history is analogous to the plot of a novel, ontology is more like a study of the novel's central characters", and that is exactly what he does, an analysis as interesting as useless of the existence of the Dutch East Indian Company, a perfect dissection full of curiosities but completely devoid of theoretical relevance. As interesting as Harman's approach might be, he takes all the risks on suggesting that all the atrocities that he doesn't want to talk about are not and shouldn't be a fundamental concern. The problem with an ontologically centered approach is that takes the attention away from what the things do, and the effects of relations; this can't be the motif of the social sciences. No matter how seductive OOO could be, if it's not political, or pretends not to be, it won't help improve the conditions we live under and will remain a frivolity of a privileged sphere. Social sciences and social theory exist for a reason, and that ain't making ontologies. It's helping understand reality so we can improve it – nothing else, nothing more.

Although I would wholeheartedly agree with OOO that the existence of objects goes beyond relations and is ontologically not defined by such relationships, and certainly not relations with humans, I argue that this is precisely the challenge of OOO if it's to be used as a philosophical base for the development of social sciences and social theory. OOO requires an adaptation to be used for social theory. The agenda of OOO can't be to produce an ontology of objects per se (Harman, 2016); that agenda works beautifully to develop the philosophical apparatus, which Harman has completed in a brilliant way, but it is useless to develop social theory embedded in political and ethical commitments. In social theory, the place of the human being and the effects of what we do to others (humans and nonhumans) can't be neglected, even if we try to produce a nonhuman-centered approach, as I do. I don't mean this in the old-fashioned way in which reality was understood as our representation of it; those days should be over soon. I mean it in the sense that especially now that we are focusing attention on processes that are not consciously driven, or in understanding other organisms like plants or animals, or thinking about climate change, an ontology of these objects, or the theorization of these objects, is useful only if it helps us improve the patterns of relations that we establish with such entities. In other words, whereas philosophy has the purpose of creating systems and concepts that allow us to better understand reality, social sciences should target the production of theory that not only helps us understand the specificities of realities, but such theories also should aim to give cues to improve these realities – again, for human beings but also for other agencies participating in the world. Therefore, politics should come first.

Digesting Reality's agenda is to infect OOO, to put some color in what I think is the whitest theory at the moment and emblem of privilege. This is precisely the one theory that needs to be taken over, corrupted. Behind my choice of alternating OOO and process philosophies lies the commitment to politicize the less political theory at the moment, precisely because there is danger in developing a brilliant theory for the wrong purposes. The politics of *Digesting Reality* craves a production of knowledge that maintains creation as the radical quality that helps us better understand the reality we live under, and in doing so, I believe it's our duty to decolonize these theories whose agendas do not improve the conditions we live under.

In a similar vein, the decision to introduce aesthetic elements like experimental writing and poetry and the decision to include insights from some sciences is motivated by a deep desire of changing the form of knowledge in twenty-first century using all available resources to create new ways of understanding new realities. Aesthetics is important to understand human life, and subjectivity is no less important as a resource to construct a different knowledge. If science has contributed so much to human affairs, it should be a matter of concern for social theory. Unsettling the ways in which we produce knowledge and challenging the alleged incompatibilities of theoretical approaches helps open possibilities and eventually creates better theories. That is what I have tried to do here: create a different theory, one that helps us better digest reality.

References

Allen-Collison, J., and Hockey, J. 2010. Feeling the Way: Notes Toward a Haptic Phenomenology of Distance Running and Scuba Diving. *International Review for the Sociology of Sport* 46 (3): 330–345.

Allen-Collinson, J., and Owton, H. 2015. Intense Embodiment: Senses of Heat in Women's Running and Boxing. *Body & Society* 21 (2): 245–268.

Anderson, B. 2009. Affective Atmospheres. *Emotion, Space and Society* 2 (2): 77–81.

Anderson, B. 2014. *Encountering Affect: Capacities, Apparatuses, Conditions*. Farnham, Surrey. Burlington, VT: Ashgate Pub Co.

Anderson, B., and Ash, J. 2015. Atmospheric Methods. In *Non-representational Methodologies*, ed. P. Vannini, 34–51. New York: Routledge.

Angerer, M. L., Bösel, B., and Ott, M. (eds.). 2014. *Timing of Affect: Epistemologies, Aesthetics, Politics*. Zurich: Diaphanes.

Ansell-Pearson, K. 2001. *Philosophy and the Adventure of the Virtual*. London: Routledge.

Barad, K. 2007. *Meeting the Universe Halfway*. Durham: Duke University Press.

Barad, K. 2010. Quantum Entanglements and Hauntological Relations of Inheritance: Dis/Continuities, SpaceTime Enfoldings, and Justice-to-Come. *Derrida Today* 3 (2): 240–268.

Barad, K. 2012. On Touching – The Inhuman That Therefore I Am. *Differences* 23 (3): 206–223.

Barad, K. 2014. Diffracting Diffraction: Cutting Together-Apart. *Parallax* 20 (3): 168–187.

Bautista, J. A., Orozco, C., and Teran, S. 2015. La disminución de la producción artesanal de mezcal en la Región del mezcal de Oaxaca, México. *Rev. Mex. Cienc. Agríc* [online] 6 (6): 1291–1305.

Behar, K. 2016. *Object-Oriented Feminism*. Minneapolis: University of Minnesota Press.

Bennett, J. 2010. *Vibrant Matter*. Durham: Duke University Press.

Bennett, J. 2012. Systems and Things: A Response to Graham Harman and Timothy Morton. *New Literary History* 43 (2): 225–233.

Bennett, J. 2015. Systems and Things: On Vital Materialism and Object-Oriented Philosophy. In *The Nonhuman Turn*, ed. Richard Grusin, 223–240. Minneapolis: University of Minnesota Press.

Bennett, T., Dodsworth, F., Noble, G., Poovey, M., and Watkins, M. 2013. Habit and Habituation: Governance and the Social. *Body & Society* 19 (2&3): 3–29.

Bentley, A. 2015. *A Cultural History of Food in the Modern Age*. New York: Bloomsbury.

Bergson, H. 1965. *Duration and Simultaneity*. New York: THE BOBBS-MERRILL COMPANY INC.

Bergson, H. 2001. *Time and Free Will*. New York: Dover Publications Inc.

Bergson, H. 2005. Matter and Memory. New York: Zone Books.

Berlant, L. 2004. *Compassion. The Culture and Politics of an Emotion*. New York: Routledge.

Berlant, L. 2011. *Cruel Optimism*. Durham: Duke University Press.

Bhardar, B., and Goldberg-Hiller, J. 2015. *Plastic Materialities*. Durham: Duke University Press.

Blackman, L. 2010. Embodying Affect: Voice-Hearing, Telepathy, Suggestion and Modelling the Nonconscious. *Body and Society* 16 (1): 163–192.

Blackman, L. 2013. Habit and Affect: Revitalizing a Forgotten History. *Body & Society* 19 (2&3): 186–216.

Blackman, L. 2014. Affect and Automaticy: Towards an Analytics of Experimentation. *Subjectivity* 7 (4): 362–384.

Blackman, L., and Venn, C. 2010. Affect. *Body and Society* 16 (1): 7–28.

Bogost, I. 2012. *Alien Phenomenology*. Minneapolis: University of Minnesota Press.

Bösel, B. 2014. Affective Synchronization, Rhythmanalysis and the Polyphonic Qualities of the Present Moment. In *Timing of Affect: Epistemologies, Aesthetics, Politics*, ed. M.-L. Angerer, B. Bösel, and M. Ott, 87–102. Zurich: Diaphanes.

Bourdieu, P. 1990. *The Logic of Practice*. Cambridge: Polity Press.

Bourdieu, P. 2005. *Outline of a Theory of Practice*. Cambridge: Cambridge University Press.

Bowen, S. 2015. *Divided Spirits. Tequila, Mezcal and the Politics of Production*. Oakland: University of California Press.

Braidotti, R. 2019. *Posthuman Knowledge*. Medford: Polity Press.

Brennan, T. 2004. *The Transmission of Affect*. Ithaca and London: Cornell University Press.

Brown, S. y Stenner, P. 2001. Being Affected: Spinoza and the Psychology of Emotion. *International Journal of Group Tensions* 30 (1): 81–105.

Brown, S., and Stenner, P. 2009. *Psychology Without Foundations: History, Philosophy and Psychosocial Theory*. London: Sage Publications Ltd.

Bryant, L. 2011. *The Democracy of Objects*. Michigan: Open Humanities Press.

Bryant, L., Srnicek, N., and Harman, G. (eds.). 2011. *The Speculative Turn: Continental Materialism and Realism*. Melbourne, VIC: Re.press.

Calvo, P., Pratap, V., and Trewavas, A. 2017. Are Plants Sentient? *Plant Cell Environ* 40: 2858–2869.

Campbell, C. 2013. *Animal vs. Plant Protein*. Available from: http://nutritionstudies.org/animal-vs-plant-protein/.

Canales, J. 2005. Einstein, Bergson, and the Experiment That Failed: Intellectual Cooperation at the League of Nations. *Modern Language Notes* 120 (5): 1168–1191.

Canales, J. 2015. *The Physicist and the Philosopher: Einstein, Bergson, and the Debate That Changed Our Understanding of Time*. S.l.: Princeton University Press.

Candas, V., and Dufour, A. 2005. Thermal Comfort: Multisensory Interactions? *Journal of Physiological Anthropology* 24: 33–36.

Castle, D., Culver, K., and Hannah, W. 2012. Scenarios for Food Security. In *The Philosophy of Food*, ed. D. Kaplan, 250–268. Berkeley: University of California Press.

Caterina, M. J., and Julius, D. 2001. The Vanilloid Receptor: A Molecular Gateway to the Pain Pathway. *Annual Review of Neuroscience* 24: 487–517.

Caterina, M. J., Rosen, T. A., Tominaga, M., Brake, A. J., and Julius, D. 1999. A Capsaicin-Receptor Homologue with a High Threshold for Noxious Heat. *Nature* 398 (6726): 436–441.

Caterina, M. J., Schumacher, M. A., Tominaga, M., Rosen, T. A., Levine, J. D., and Julius, D. 1997. The Capsaicin Receptor: A Heat-activated Ion Channel in the Pain Pathway. *Nature* 389 (6653): 816–824.

Chamovitz, D. 2017. *What a Plant Knows*. New York: Scientific American/Farrar, Straus and Giroux.

Classen, C. 1993. *Worlds of Sense*. New York: Routledge.

Classen, C., Howes, D., and Synnott, A. 1994. *Aroma. The Cultural History of Smell*. London: Routledge.

Clough, P. 2004. Future Matters: Techno-science, Global Politics, and Cultural Criticism. *Social Text* 22 (3): 1–23.

Clough, P. 2008. The Affective Turn. Political Economy, Biomedia and Bodies. *Theory, Culture and Society* 25 (1): 1–22.

Clough, P. 2010. Afterword: The Future of Affect Studies. *Body & Society* 16 (1): 222–230

Clough, P. 2012. Feminist Theory: Bodies, Science and Technology. In *Handbook of the Body*, ed. B. Turner, 95–105. London: Routledge.

Clough, P. 2014. Foreword. In *Desire After Affect*, ed. M.-L. Angerer, ix–xv. London: Rowman & Littlefield International, Ltd.

Clough, P. 2018. *The User Unconsciosus*. Minneapolis: Minnesota University Press.

Clough, P., and Halley, J. (eds.). 2007. *The Affective Turn: Theorizing the Social*. Durham, NC: Duke University Press Books.

Clough, P., and Wisley, C. (eds.). (2011). *Beyond Biopolitics. Essays on Governance of Life and Death*. Durham: Duke University Press.

Coe, S., and Coe, M. 2013. *The True History of Chocolate*. London: Thames & Hudson.

Coetzee, M. 1999. *The Lives of Animals*. Princeton, NJ: Princeton University Press.

Coole, D., and Frost, S. (eds.). 2010. *New Materialisms: Ontology, Agency, and Politics*. Durham: Duke University Press.

Connolly, W. 2002. *Neuropolitics*. Minneapolis: Minnesota University Press.

Coveney, J. 2000. *Food, Morals and Meaning: The Pleasure and Anxiety of Eating*. London: Taylor & Francis.

Cromby, J. 2007. Integrating Social Science with Neuroscience: Potentials and Problems. *BioSocieties* 2 (2): 149–169.

Cromby, J., Newton, T., and Williams, S. 2011. Neurosciences and Subjectivity. *Subjectivity* 4: 215–226.

Damasio, A. 2003. *Looking for Spinoza: Joy, Sorrow, and the Feeling Brain*. New York: Harvest.

Damasio, A. 2010. *Self Comes to Mind: Constructing the Conscious Brain*. New York: Vintage Books.

Dean, J. 2000. *Cultural Studies and Political Theory*. New York: Cornell University Press.

Delanda, M. 2016. *Assemblage Theory*. Edinburgh: Edinburgh University Press.

Deleuze, G. 1988. *Spinoza: Practical Philosophy*. San Francisco: City Lights.

Deleuze, G. 1997. Desire and Pleasure. In *Foucault and His Interlocutors*, ed. A. Davidson, 183–192. Chicago: The University of Chicago Press.

Deleuze, G. 2011. *Bergsonism*. New York: Zone Books.

Deleuze, G., and Guattari, F. 1977. *Anti-Oedipus. Capitalism and Schizophrenia*. New York: Penguin Classics.

Deleuze, G., and Guattari, F. 1987. *A Thousand Plateaus*. Minneapolis: University of Minnesota Press.

Deleuze, G., and Guattari, F. 1994. *What Is Philosophy?* New York: Columbia University Press.

Despret, V. 2004. The Body We Care for: Figures of Anthropo-Zoo-Genesis. *Body & Society* 10 (2–3): 111–134.

Dingle, H. 1965. Introduction. In *Duration and Simultaneity*, ed. H. Bergon, XV–XIV. New York: The Bobbs-Merrill Company, Inc.

Einstein, A. 1987. *Letters to Solovine*. New York: Philosophical Library.

Enciso, G., and Lara, A. 2014. Emociones y Ciencias Sociales en el s. XX: La precuela del Giro Afectivo. *Athenea Digital – Revista de Pensamiento E Investigacio'n Social* 14 (1): 263–288.

Englen, L. 2012. Oral Receptors. In *Food Oral Processing: Fundamentals of Eating and Sensory Perception*, eds. J. Chen and L. Engelen, 15–43. Sussex: Wiley Blackwell.

Fitzgerald, D., and Callard, F. 2014. Social Science and Neuroscience Beyond Interdisciplinarity: Experimental Entanglements. *Theory, Culture and Society*, 31 (2): 3–31.

Frost, S. 2016. *Biocultural Creatures. Toward a New Theory of the Human*. Durham: Duke University Press.

García-Garza, D. 2010. Prácticas alimenticias y clasificación social. ¿Los tacos son un alimento ¿popular? *Civitas – Revista de Ciências Sociais* 10 (3): 430–449.

García Garza, D. 2011. Una etnografía económica de los tacos callejeros en México. El caso de Monterrey. *Estudios Sociales* 19 (37): 32–63.

Gard, M. 2009. Understanding Obesity by Understanding Desire. In *Critical Feminist Approaches to Eating Dis/orders*, eds. H. Malson and M. Burns, 35–45. New York: Routledge.

Gatens, M. 2014. Affective Transitions and Spinoza's Art of Joyful Deliberation. In *Timing of Affect: Epistemologies, Aesthetics, Politics*, eds. M.-L. Angerer, B. Bösel, and M. Ott, 17–33. Zurich: Diaphanes.

Giddens, A. 1979. *Central Problems in Social Theory*. Berkeley: University of California Press.

Giddens, A. 1984. *The Constitution of Society*. Berkeley: University of California Press.

Goodman, S. 2010. *Sonic Warfare: Sound, Affect, and the Ecology of Fear*. Cambridge, MA: The MIT Press.

Gottlieb, R., and Joshi, A. 2010. *Food Justice*. Cambridge: The MIT Press.

Greene, G. 2017. *The Mezcal Rush. Exploration in Agave Country*. Berkeley: Counterpoint.

Greenebaum, J. 2012. Veganism, Identity and the Quest for Authenticity. *Food, Culture and Society* 15: 129–144.

Gregg, M., and Seigworth, G. 2010. *The Affect Theory Reader*. Durham: Duke University Press.

Gross, J., and Grosenberger, N. 2010. The Double Binds of Getting Food Among the Poor in Rural Oregon. *Food, Culture & Society* 13 (1): 47–70.

Grosz, E. 2004. *The Nick of Time: Politics, Evolution, and the Untimely*. Durham: Duke University Press.

Grusin, R. (ed.). 2015. *The Nonhuman Turn*. Minneapolis: University of Minnesota Press.

Guthman, J. 2011. *Weighing in, Obesity, Food Justice and the Limits of Capitalism*. Los Angeles: University of California Press.

Hansen, M. B. N. 2006. *New Philosophy for New Media*. Cambridge, MA: MIT Press.

Hansen, M. B. N. 2014. Feelings Without Feelers, or Affective as Environmental Force. In *Timing of Affect: Epistemologies, Aesthetics, Politics*, ed. M.-L. Angerer, B. Bošel, and M. Ott, 65–86. Zurich: Diaphanes.

Hansen, M. B. N. 2015. *Feed-Froward. On the Future of Twenty-First Century Media*. London: University of Chicago Press.

Harman, G. 2005. *Guerrilla Metaphysics*. Illinois: Open Court.

Harman, G. 2011a. *The Quadruple Object*. Washington: Zero books.

Harman, G. 2011b. Response to Shaviro. In *The Speculative Turn*, eds. L. Bryant, N. Srnicek, and G. Harman, 291–333. New York: Re.press.

Harman, G. 2012. The Well-Wrought Broken Hammer. *New Literary History* 43 (2): 183–203.

Harman, G. 2016. *Immaterialism: Objects and Social Theory*. Cambridge, UK: Polity Press.

Harman, G. 2018. *Object-Oriented Ontology. A New Theory of Everything*. London: Pelican Books.

Havlicek, J., and Lenochova, P. 2008. Environmental Effects on Human Body Odour. In *Chemical Signals in Vertebrates 11*, ed. J. Hurst, 199–211. New York: Springer.

Hayles, K. 1999. *How We Became Posthuman*. Chicago: The University of Chicago Press.

Hayles, K. 2017. *Unthought. The Power of the Cognitive Nonconscious*. Chicago: The University of Chicago Press.

Hennion, A. 2007. Those Things That Hold Us Together: Taste and Sociology. *Cultural Sociology* 1 (1): 97–114.

Henriques, J. et al. 1984. *Changing the Subject: Psychology, Social Regulation and Subjectivity*. London: Routledge.

Henriques, J., Tiainen, M., and Va'liaho, P. 2014. Rhythm Returns: Movement and Cultural Theory. *Body and Society* 20 (3–4): 3–29.

Henshaw, J. 2012. *A Tour of the Senses*. Baltimore: Johns Hopkins University Press.

Hui Kyong Chun, W. 2017. *Updating to Remain the Same. Habitual New Media*. Cambridge: The MIT Press.

Ingold, T. 2011. *Being Alive: Essays in Movement, Knowledge, and Description*. London: Routledge.

Ikoniadou, E. 2014. Abstract Time and Affective Perception in the Sonic Work of Art. *Body and Society* 20 (3–4): 140–161.

Jablonski, N. 2006. *Skin: A Natural History*. Berkeley: University of California Press.

Jancso, N. 1967. Direct Evidence for Neurogenic Inflammation and Its Prevention by Denervation and by Pretreatment With Capsaicin. *Pharmacol Chemother* 31 (1): 138–151.

Janzen, E. 2017. *Mezcal. The History, Craft & Cocktails of the World's Ultimate Spirit*. Minneapolis: Voyageur Press.

Jallinoja, P., Pajari, P., and Absetz, P. 2010. Negotiated Pleasures in Health-seeking Lifestyles of Participants of a Health Promoting Intervention. *Health* 14 (2): 115–130.

Jordt, S.-E., and Julius, D. 2002. Molecular Basis for Species-Specific Sensitivity to "Hot" Chili Peppers. *Cell* 108 (3): 421–430.

Julier, A. 2013. The Political Economy of Obesity: The Fat Pay All. In *Food and Culture*, eds. C. Counihan and P. Van Esterik, 546–562. London: Routledge.

Kohn, E. 2013. *How Forests Think. Toward an Anthropology Beyond the Human*. Berkeley: University of California Press.

Kolozova, K., and Joy, E. 2016. *After the "Speculative Turn" Realism, Philosophy and Feminism*. San Bernandino: Punctum Books.

Krause, S. 2015. *Freedom Beyond Sovereignty. Reconstructing Liberal Individualism*. Chicago, IL: University of Chicago Press.

Lagiou, P. et al. 2012. Low Carbohydrate-high Protein Diet and Incidence of Cardiovascular Diseases in Swedish Women: Prospective Cohort Study. *MBJ* 344.

Landecker, H. 2007. *Culturing Life: How Cells Became Technology*. Cambridge: Harvard University Press.

Landecker, H. 2011. Food as Exposure: Nutritional Epigenetics and the New Metabolism. *BioSocieties* 6 (2): 167–194.

Lara, A. 2015. Teorías Afectivas Vintage. Apuntes sobre Deleuze, Bergson y Whitehead. Cinta de Moebio. *Revista de Epistemología de Ciencias Sociales* 52: 17–36.

Lara, A., and Enciso, G. 2014. Ciencia, Teoría Social y Cuerpo en el Giro Afectivo: Esferas de Articulación. *Quaderns de Psicologia* 16 (2): 7–25.

Lara, A., Liu, W., Ashley, C., Nishida, A., Liebert, R., and Bilies, M. 2017. Affect & Subjectivity. *Subjectivity* 10 (1): 30–43.

Latour, B. 2004. How to Talk About the Body? The Normative Dimension of Science Studies. *Body and Society* 10 (2–3): 205–229.

Latour, B., and Eliasson, O. 2011. Revisiting the DEBATE Between Bergson and Einstein. Presented at the Three Days of Making Time: Revisiting the Debate Between Bergson and Einstein, Berlin.

Lavin, C. 2013. *Eating Anxiety. The Perils of Food Politics*. Minneapolis: University of Minnesota Press.

Lee, H., Carstens, E., and O'Mahony, M. 2003. Drinking Hot Coffee: Why Doesn't It Burn the Mouth. *Journal of Sensory Studies* 18: 19–32.

LeDoux, J. 1998. *The Emotional Brain: The Mysterious Underpinnings of Emotional Life*. New York: Simon & Schuster.

Leys, R. 2007. *From Guilt to Shame: Auschwitz and After*. Princeton: Princeton University Press.

Leys, R. 2011. The Turn to Affect: A Critique. *Critical Inquiry* 37 (7): 434–472.

Lowry, M. 1947. *Under the Volcano*. London: Penguin Books.

Malabou, C. 2008. *What Should We Do with Our Brain?* New York: Fordham University Press.

Malabou, C. 2012. *Ontology of the Accident*. Malden: Polity Press.

Malabou, C. 2015. Will Sovereignty Ever Be Deconstructed? In *Plastic Materialities*, eds. B. Bhardar and J. Goldberg-Hiller, 35–46. Durham: Duke University Press.

Mancuso, S. 2018. *The Revolutionary Genius of Plants*. New York: Atria Books.

Manning, E., and Massumi, B. 2014. *Thought in the Act: Passages in the Ecology of Experience*. Minneapolis: University of Minnesota Press.

Martin. 2010.

Massumi, B. 1992. *A User's Guide to Capitalism and Schizophrenia*. Cambridge, MA: The MIT Press.

Massumi, B. 2002. *Parables for the Virtual*. Durham: Duke University Press.

Massumi, B. 2015a. *Ontopower. War, Powers and the State of Perception*. Durham: Duke University Press.

Massumi, B. 2015b. *Politics of Affect*. Malden: Polity Press.

McPhail, P., Beagan, B., and Chapman, G. 2012. "I Don't Want to Be Sexist but . . ." Denying and Re-Inscribing Gender Through Food. *Food, Culture & Society* 15 (3): 473–489.

Meillassoux, Q. 2008. *After Finitude: An Essay on the Necessity of Contingency*. New York: Continuum.

Miller, J., and Deutsch, J. 2014. *Food Studies. An Introduction to Research Methods*. London: Bloomsbury.

Mol, A. 2012. Mind Your Plate! The Ontonorms of Dutch dieting. *Social Studies of Science* 43 (3): 379–396.

Mol, A. 2013a. Mind Your Plate! The Ontonorms of Dutch Dieting. *Social Studies of Science* 43 (3): 379–396.

Mol, A. 2013b. Language Trails: 'Lekker' and Its Pleasures. *Theory, Culture & Society* 3 (2/3): 93–119.

Moran, V. 1985. *Compassion the Ultimate Ethic. An Exploration of Veganism*. Northamptonshire: Thorsons Publishers Limited.

Morton, T. 2009. *Ecology Without Nature. Rethinking Environmental Aesthetics*. Cambridge: Harvard University Press.

Morton, T. 2012. An Object-Oriented Defense of Poetry. *New Literary History* 43 (2): 205–224.

Morton, T. 2013a. *Hyperobjects*. Minneapolis: Minnesota University Press.

Morton, T. 2013b. *Realist Magic*. Michigan: Open Humanities Press.

Morton, T. 2016. *Dark Ecology. For a Logic of Future Coexistence*. New York: Columbia University Press.

Nassbaum, M. 2001. *Upheavals of Thought: The Intelligence of Emotions.* New York: Cambridge University Press.

Ngai, S. 2005. *Ugly Feelings*. Cambridge: Harvard University Press.

Ong, B. 2012. Warming Up to Heat. *Senses & Society* 7 (1): 5–21.

O'Connell, J. 2011. *Sugar Nation: The Hidden Truth Behind America's Deadliest Habit and the Simple Way to Beat It*. New York: Hachette Books.

O'Rouke, M. 2011. Girls Welcome!!! Speculative Realism, Object-Oriented Ontology and Queer Theory. *Speculations* II: 275–312.

Ospina, W. 2003. *Poesía Reunida*. Bogotà: Lumen.

Paddon-Jones, D. et al. 2015. Protein and Healthy Aging. *American Society for Nutrition*101 (6): 1339S–1345S.

Panagia, D. 2009. *The Political Life of Sensation*. Durham: Duke University Press.

Parisi, L. 2004. *Abstract Sex: Philosophy, Biotechnology and the Mutations of Desire*. London & New York: Continuum.

Parisi, L. 2013. *Contagious Architecture: Computation, Aesthetics, and Space*. Cambridge, MA: The MIT Press.

Parisi, L., and Terranova, T. 2000. *Heat-Death, Emergence and Control in Genetic Engineering and Artificial Life. Ctheory* [online]. Available from: www.ctheory.net/articles.aspx?id=127 [Accessed March 2015].

Papoulias, C., and Callard, F. 2010. Biology's Gift. *Body & Society* 16 (1): 29–56.

Pawlak, R. et al. 2013. How Prevalent Is Vitamin B12 Deficiency Among Vegetarians? *Nutrition Reviews* 71 (2): 110–117.

Pilchner, J. M. 2012. *Planet Taco: A Global History of Mexican Food*. New York: Oxford University Press.

Pitts-Taylor, V. 2013. I Feel Your Pain: Embodied Knowledges and Situated Neurons. *Hypatia: A Journal of Feminist Philosophy* 28 (4): 852–869.

Pitts-Taylor, V. 2016. *The Brain's Body*. Durham: Duke University Press.

Potter, C. 2008. Sense of Motion, Senses of Self: Becoming a Dancer. *Ethos* 73 (4): 444–465.

Potts, A., and Parry, J. 2010. Vegan Sexuality: Challenging Heteronormative Masculinity Through Meat-free Sex. *Feminism & Psychology* 20 (1): 53–72.

Prigogine, I., and Stengers, I. 1984. *Order Out of Chaos, Man's New Dialogue with Nature*. New York: Bantam Books.

Probyn, E. 2000. *Carnal Appetites: Foodsexidentities*. London: Routledge.

Probyn, E. 2009. Fat, Feelings, Bodies: A Critical Approach to Obesity. In *Critical Feminist Approaches to Eating Dis/orders*, eds. H. Malson and M. Burns, 113–123. London: Routledge.

Probyn, E. 2012. In the Interests of Taste & Place: Economies of Attachment. In *The Global and the Intimate: Feminism in Our Time*, eds. G. Pratt and V. Rosner, 57–84. New York: Columbia University Press.

Protevi, J. 2009. *Political Affect, Connecting the Social and the Somatic.* Minneapolis: University of Minnesota Press.

Rabinbach, A. 1992. *The Human Motor: Energy, Fatigue, and the Origins of Modernity.* Los Angeles: University of California Press.

Rancière, J. 2014. *Dissensus. On Politics and Aesthetics.* London: Bloomsbury.

Reckwitz, A. 2002. Toward a Theory of Social Practices: A Development in Culturalist Theorizing. *European Journal of Social Theory* 5 (2): 243–263.

Rizzolatti, G., and Craighero, L. 2004. The Mirror Neuron System. *Annual Review of Neuroscineces* 27 (1): 169–192.

Roberts, S. et al. 2005. Body Odor Similarity in Noncohabiting Twins. *Chem. Senses* 30: 651–656.

Rozin, P. 1999. Food Is Fundamental, Fun, Frightening, and Far-reaching. *Social Research* 66 (1): 9–30.

Sampson, T. 2017. *The Assemblage Brain. Sense Making in Neuroculture.* Minneapolis: University of Minnesota Press.

Schatzki, T., Knorr Cetina, K., and Savigny, E. 2001. *The Practice Turn in Contemporary Theory.* London: Routledge.

Schellnhuber, H., Cramer, W., Nakicenovic, N., and Wigley, T. 2006. *Avoiding Dangerous Climate Change.* New York: Cambridge University Press.

Schwartz, J., and Bagley, S. 2002. *The Mind and the Brain: Neuronal Plasticity and the Power of Mental Force.* New York: HarperCollins.

Shaviro, S. 2011. The Actual Volcano: Whitehead, Harman, and the Problem of Relations. In *The Speculative Turn. Continental Materialism and Realism*, eds. I. Bryant, N. Srnicek, and G. Harman, 279–290. Melbourne: Re-press.

Shaviro, S. 2014a. *The Universe of Things: On Speculative Realism.* Minneapolis: University of Minnesota Press.

Shaviro, S. 2014b. Discognition. In *Timing of Affect: Epistemologies, Aesthetics, Politics*, eds. M.-L. Angerer, B. Bösel, and M. Ott, 49–64. Zurich: Diaphanes.

Shaviro, S. 2015. *No Speed Limit. Three Essays on Accelerationism.* Minneapolis: University of Minnesota Press.

Shaviro, S. 2016. *Discognition.* London: Repeater.

Sheldon, R. 2015. Form/Matter/Chora: Object-Oriented Ontology and Feminist New Materialism. In *The Nonhuman Turn*, ed. R. Grusin, 193–222. Minneapolis: Minnesota University Press.

Shepherd, G. 2013. *Neurogastronomy: How the Brain Creates Flavor and Why It Matters.* New York: Columbia University Press.

Smith, M., and Morra, J. 2006. *The Prosthetic Impulse. From a Posthuman Present to a Biocultural Future.* Cambridge: The MIT Press.

Sokal, A. D., and Bricmont, J. 1998. *Fashionable Nonsense: Postmodern Intellectuals' Abuse of Science.* New York: Picador USA.

Sparrow, T. 2014. *Plastic Bodies: Rebuilding Sensation After Phenomenology.* London: Open Humanities Press.

Standage, T. 2006. *A History of the World in Six Glasses.* New York: Walker Publishing Company.

Stenner, P. 2008. A.N. Whitehead and Subjectivity. *Subjectivity* 22 (1): 90–109.

Stenner, P., and Greco, M. 2013. Affectivity. *Informática na educacão: teoria & prática* 16 (1): 49–70.

Stenner, P., and Moreno, E. 2013. Liminality and Affectivity: The Case of Deceased Organ Donation. *Subjectivity* 6 (3): 229–253.

Stern, D. 2000. *The Interpersonal World of the Infant: A View from Psychoanalysis and Developmental Psychology*. New York: Basic Books.

Stearns, P. N., and Stearns, C. Z. 1985. Emotionology: Clarifying the History of Emotions and Emotional Standards. *The American Historical Review* 90 (4): 813–836.

Stewart, K. 2011. Atmospheric Attunements. *Environment and Planning D: Society and Space* 29 (3): 445–453.

Szakolczai, A. 2009. Liminality and Experience: Structuring Transitory Situations and Transformative Events. *International Political Anthropology* 2 (1): 141–172.

Tellez, Z. 2011. *Picante y capsaícina. Letras libres video* [online]. Available from: www.youtube.com/watch?v=5Z0b-V4k3OKY&feature=youtube_gdata_player.

Thompson, M., and Biddle, I. (eds.). 2013. *Sound, Music, Affect: Theorizing Sonic Experience*. New York: Bloomsbury Academic.

Thompson, P., and Hoggett, S. 2012. *Politics and the Emotions. The Affective Turn in Contemporary Political Studies*. New York: Continuum.

Turin, L. 2007. *The Secret of Scent*. New York: Harper Perennial.

Turner, B. 1996. *The Body and Society: Explorations in Social Theory*. London: Sage.

Tuso, F. et al. 2013. Nutritional Update for Physicians: Plant-Based Diets. *The Permanent Journal* 17 (2): 61–66.

Ure, M., and Frost, M. 2014. *The Politics of Compassion*. New York: Routledge.

Vannini, P. (ed.). 2015. *Non-representational Methodologies: Re-envisioning Research*. New York: Routledge.

Vannini, P., and Taggart, J. 2014a. Making Sense of Domestic Warmth Affect, Involvement, and Thermoception in Off-grid Homes. *Body & Society* 20 (1): 61–84.

Vannini, P., and Taggart, J. 2014b. Food, Culture and Society: An International Journal of Multidisciplinary Research. *Food, Culture & Society* 17 (2): 319–336.

Vardi, I. 2010. Feeding Race. *Food, Culture & Society* 13 (3): 371–396.

Vogel, E., and Mol, A. 2014. Enjoy Your Food: On Losing Weight and Taking Pleasure. *Sociology of Health & Illness* 36 (2): 305–317.

Watson, J., and Caldwell, L. 2005. *The Cultural Politics of Food and Eating*. Malden: Blackwell Publishing.

Wetherell, M. 2012. *Affect and Emotions. A New Social Understanding*. London: Sage ltd.

Wetherell, M. 2013. Affect and Discourse – What's the Problem? From Affect as Excess to Affective/Discursive Practice. *Subjectivity* 6 (4): 349–368.

Wetherell, M. 2015. Trends in the Turn to Affect: A Social Psychological Critique. *Body & Society* 21 (2): 139–166.

Willson, M. 2005. Indulgence. In *Fat*, eds. D. Kulik and A. Menely, 153–167. New York: Tarcher/Penguin.

Whitehead, A. N. 1919. *The Concept of Nature*. Cambridge: Cambridge University Press.

Whitehead, A. N. 1985. *Process and Reality*. New York: Free Press.
Whitfort, D. 2005. *Proteins: Structure and Function*. Sussex: John Wiley & Sons Ltd.
Whrangham, R. 2010. *Catching Fire. How Cooking Make Us Human*. New York: Basic Books.
Wright, L. 2015. *The Vegan Studies Project. Food, Animals and Gender in the Age of Terror*. Athens: University of Georgia Press.

Index

For Product Safety Concerns and Information please contact our EU
representative GPSR@taylorandfrancis.com
Taylor & Francis Verlag GmbH, Kaufingerstraße 24, 80331 München, Germany

www.ingramcontent.com/pod-product-compliance
Ingram Content Group UK Ltd.
Pitfield, Milton Keynes, MK11 3LW, UK
UKHW022109190926
475702UK00013B/1347
* 9 7 8 0 3 6 7 5 3 4 8 5 1 *